P9-DFZ-864

CHESAPEAKE COLLEGE
THE LIBRARY
WYE MILLS,
MARYLAND 21679

New Directions for
Teaching and Learning

Catherine M. Wehlburg
EDITOR-IN-CHIEF

Hidden Roads: Nonnative English-Speaking International Professors in the Classroom

Katherine Grace Hendrix
Aparna Hebbani

EDITORS

Number 138 • Summer 2014
Jossey-Bass
San Francisco

LB
1778.2
.H533
2014

Hidden Roads: Nonnative English-Speaking International Professors in the Classroom
Katherine Grace Hendrix, Aparna Hebbani (eds.)
New Directions for Teaching and Learning, no. 138
Catherine M. Wehlburg, Editor-in-Chief

Copyright © 2014 Wiley Periodicals, Inc., A Wiley Company. All rights reserved. No part of this publication may be reproduced, stored in a retrieval system, or transmitted in any form or by any means, electronic, mechanical, photocopying, recording, scanning, or otherwise, except as permitted under Section 107 or 108 of the 1976 United States Copyright Act, without either the prior written permission of the Publisher or authorization through payment of the appropriate per-copy fee to the Copyright Clearance Center, 222 Rosewood Drive, Danvers, MA 01923, (978) 750-8400, fax (978) 646-8600. Requests to the Publisher for permission should be addressed to the Permissions Department, c/o John Wiley & Sons, Inc., 111 River St., Hoboken, NJ 07030; (201) 748-8789, fax (201) 748-6326, http://www.wiley.com/go/permissions.

Microfilm copies of issues and articles are available in 16 mm and 35 mm, as well as microfiche in 105 mm, through University Microfilms, Inc., 300 North Zeeb Road, Ann Arbor, MI 48106-1346.

NEW DIRECTIONS FOR TEACHING AND LEARNING (ISSN 0271-0633, electronic ISSN 1536-0768) is part of The Jossey-Bass Higher and Adult Education Series and is published quarterly by Wiley Subscription Services, Inc., A Wiley Company, at Jossey-Bass, One Montgomery Street, Suite 1200, San Francisco, CA 94104-4594. POSTMASTER: Send address changes to New Directions for Teaching and Learning, Jossey-Bass, One Montgomery Street, Suite 1200, San Francisco, CA 94104-4594.

New Directions for Teaching and Learning is indexed in CIJE: Current Index to Journals in Education (ERIC), Contents Pages in Education (T&F), Educational Research Abstracts Online (T&F), ERIC Database (Education Resources Information Center), Higher Education Abstracts (Claremont Graduate University), and SCOPUS (Elsevier).

INDIVIDUAL SUBSCRIPTION RATE (in USD): $89 per year US/Can/Mex, $113 rest of world; institutional subscription rate: $311 US, $351 Can/Mex, $385 rest of world. Single copy rate: $29. Electronic only–all regions: $89 individual, $311 institutional; Print & Electronic–US: $98 individual, $357 institutional; Print & Electronic–Can/Mex: $98 individual, $397 institutional; Print & Electronic–rest of world: $122 individual, $431 institutional.

EDITORIAL CORRESPONDENCE should be sent to the editor-in-chief, Catherine M. Wehlburg, c.wehlburg@tcu.edu.

www.josseybass.com

Contents

EDITORS' NOTES   1
Katherine Grace Hendrix, Aparna Hebbani

1. "Are You an Immigrant?": Identity-Based Critical   5
Reflections of Teaching Intercultural Communication
Yea-Wen Chen
This chapter examines the identity negotiations of a female international faculty of color teaching an intercultural communication course.

2. College Is Not a Restaurant: Challenging Cultural   17
Hegemony in the US Classroom
Juraj Kittler
The author offers an experience of a professor who sees his nonnative status as an opportunity to challenge existing cultural assumptions in the US classroom.

3. Rapport and Knowledge: Enhancing Foreign Instructor   29
Credibility in the Classroom
Mei Zhang
This chapter emphasizes rapport and knowledge to build instructor credibility in the oral communication class.

4. Open and Positive Attitudes toward Teaching   41
Chia-Fang (Sandy) Hsu
A teacher's willingness to work out problems with individual students, coupled with openness to students' ideas and criticism, should help improve students' negative attitudes toward the teacher. Better learning outcomes and teaching evaluations can also follow.

5. Opposite Worlds, Singular Mission: Teaching as an ITA   51
Consolata Nthemba Mutua
Teaching in a new pedagogical context and cultural milieu offers unique challenges and insight that can enhance our understanding of the American classroom experience.

6. Capturing the Experiences of International Teaching
Assistants in the US American Classroom   61

Aparna Hebbani, Katherine Grace Hendrix

The perceptions of PhD- and MA-level international teaching assistants toward their US American undergraduates are investigated. The findings of these ITAs teaching communication courses are discussed and one coauthor provides her reflexive voice as a nonnative English speaker teaching American students.

7. International Instructor Preparing Teachers for
Multicultural Classrooms in the United States: Teaching
Intercultural Communication Competence Online   73

Claudia L. McCalman

Recent demographic changes in the United States contribute to our increasing number of multicultural classrooms. Some teachers feel they need to be further prepared to effectively teach and understand challenges of multicultural classrooms. This chapter addresses perceptions and reflections of such teachers while receiving intercultural training, part of their ESL (English as a Second Language) certification. The instructor's reflections close the chapter.

8. Talking Back: Shifting the Discourse of Deficit to a Pedagogy
of Cultural Wealth of International Instructors in US
Classrooms   83

Gust A. Yep

In addition to highlighting the importance of the voices of international instructors in US classrooms, this chapter proposes a shift from the current discourse of deficit to one of cultural wealth and explores some directions for future research with this population.

INDEX   93

FROM THE SERIES EDITOR

About This Publication

Since 1980, *New Directions for Teaching and Learning* (NDTL) has brought a unique blend of theory, research, and practice to leaders in postsecondary education. NDTL sourcebooks strive not only for solid substance but also for timeliness, compactness, and accessibility.

The series has four goals: to inform readers about current and future directions in teaching and learning in postsecondary education, to illuminate the context that shapes these new directions, to illustrate these new direction through examples from real settings, and to propose ways in which these new directions can be incorporated into still other settings.

This publication reflects the view that teaching deserves respect as a high form of scholarship. We believe that significant scholarship is conducted not only by researchers who report results of empirical investigations but also by practitioners who share disciplinary reflections about teaching. Contributors to NDTL approach questions of teaching and learning as seriously as they approach substantive questions in their own disciplines, and they deal not only with pedagogical issues but also with the intellectual and social context in which these issues arise. Authors deal on the one hand with theory and research and on the other with practice, and they translate from research and theory to practice and back again.

About This Volume

Hidden Roads: Nonnative English-Speaking International Professors in the Classroom is an important publication as it foregrounds the experiences and the issues related to faculty for whom English is not their primary language. International faculty are increasing on US institutions for higher education and yet, there has not been a great deal of focus or information about their experiences. These voices are an important part of post-secondary education and special issue editors Dr. Katherine Grace Hendrix and Dr. Aparna Hebbani allow them to share their stories and help to guide higher education through these years of international and global change.

Catherine M. Wehlburg
Editor-in-Chief

Editors' Notes

International teaching faculty in the communication classroom constitute an important part of instructional staff at many US American universities. They are mostly employed as either International Teaching Assistants (ITAs who are master's or PhD students) or in the tenure-track stream as faculty. With the exception of several dissertations (Holland 2008; Kozlova 2008; Trebing 2007) and a few recent publications (Hao 2009; Hendrix 2007; Hendrix, Hebbani, and Johnson 2007; Wong (Lau) 2004; Yook and Albert 1999), much of the research on international faculty in the classroom has focused on gathering voices of US American students as the subjects (Hsu 2012; Li, Mazer, and Ju 2011; Liu, Sellnow, and Venette 2006; Zhang et al. 2007). Hence, there is a notable absence in the literature of voices of the nonnative English speaker in the classroom (that is, the ITA/International Professor) just as this was once the case for native English speakers of color—for example, African-American professors (Hendrix 1998; Jackson and Hendrix 2003).

Gathering such data through autoethnographies allows the voice of these international faculty into the chorus (Hendrix 2010). With autoethnographic research, the investigator is the epistemological and ontological nexus upon which the process turns (Spry 2001) with performative autoethnography being "critically reflexive" and, as such, providing scaffolding for contemplating "the ways in which our personal lives intersect, collide, and commune with others in the body politic" (Spry 2013, 217). According to Reed-Danahay (1997), while the emphasis on *graphy* may vary, the authors will use their own experiences to understand their interactions within a culture. She further articulates autoethnography as a genre of research and writing that connects the personal to the cultural and places the self within a social context. Ellis and Bochner (2000) describe this method as writing that "makes the researcher's own experience a topic of investigation in its own right rather than seeming as if they're written from nowhere by nobody" (734). This volume is "an invitation to dialogue" and we argue that recognizing the existence of the international professor as a classroom teacher is a first step that can ultimately lead to an investigation of research topics of interest allowing us to discover whether these faculty fall into the same "bias" bind as their African-American and Latino-American counterparts in conjunction with the assets they bring to the US classroom.

Thus, the purpose of this volume is to collate papers that address this underresearched dimension of the international faculty experience with the hope of promoting greater understanding of their classroom encounters and the pedagogical practices that ensue based on their responsibility to demonstrate subject matter expertise while simultaneously facilitating the learning

New Directions for Teaching and Learning, no. 138, Summer 2014 © 2014 Wiley Periodicals, Inc.
Published online in Wiley Online Library (wileyonlinelibrary.com) • DOI: 10.1002/tl.20091

process of US American students. Our immediate goal is to acknowledge the existence of nonnative English-speaking ITAs/professors in the classroom, thereby leading the way toward initiating more research, deliberation, and professional development centered around the needs (and assets) of these important educators who, until now, have journeyed along a hidden road leading from ITA to tenure-track faculty member.

The volume opens with Chen deftly analyzing the negotiation of co-cultural identities, including the role of race, in the intercultural classroom. In the second chapter, Kittler describes two educational systems colliding in the classroom—his European (specifically Czechoslovakian) orientation to the roles of teacher and student in contrast with the perceptions of his US American students. In the third and fourth chapters, Zhang and Hsu discuss their experiences from teaching different classes and students' experiences with nonnative speaking teachers with Zhang focusing on the intercultural dynamics and Hsu articulating how confirming behaviors have allowed her to reduce misunderstandings between professor and student. Mutua conveys her experience as an ITA in the classroom while Hebbani looks back on her crossing from ITA to tenure-track lecturer while reporting the results of an empirical study of ITAs coresearched with Hendrix. In the seventh chapter, McCalman addresses the growing English as a Second Language classroom and training US American teachers through the experiences, education, and standpoint of an international professor. Finally, the epilogue provides an opportunity for Yep to retrace the steps of these journeyers, comparing and contrasting them with travels of his own, and plotting a potential map for us to follow in the future.

Katherine Grace Hendrix
Aparna Hebbani
Editors

References

Ellis, C., and A. P. Bochner. 2000. "Autoethnography, Personal Narrative, Reflexivity: Researcher as Subject." In *Handbook of Qualitative Research*, edited by N. K. Denzin and Y. S. Lincoln, 2nd ed., 733–768. Thousand Oaks, CA: Sage.

Hao, R. N. 2009. "Finding Spirituality through Confrontation and Celebration of Asianness in the Classroom." In *As the Spirit Moves Us: Embracing Spirituality in the Postsecondary Experience*, New Directions for Teaching and Learning, no. 120, edited by K. G. Hendrix and J. D. Hamlet, 47–54. San Francisco, CA: Jossey-Bass.

Hendrix, K. G. 1998. "Black and White Male Professor Perceptions of the Influence of Race on Classroom Dynamics and Credibility." *Negro Educational Review* 49: 37–52.

Hendrix, K. G., ed. 2007. *Neither White Nor Male: The Inter/Cross-Cultural Experiences of Female Faculty of Color in Academia*, New Directions in Teaching and Learning, no. 110. San Francisco, CA: Jossey-Bass.

Hendrix, K. G. 2010. "Dialoguing with the 'Communication Chorus': Mapping the Contours of 'the Morass.'" *Southern Communication Journal* 75: 127–136.

Hendrix, K. G., A. Hebbani, and O. Johnson. 2007. "The 'Other' TA: An Exploratory Investigation of Graduate Teaching Assistants of Color (GTACs)." In *International and Intercultural Communication Annual: Communication Within/Across Organizations*, edited by B. J. Allen, L. A. Flores, and M. P. Orbe, 51–82. Washington, DC: National Communication Association.

Holland, B. 2008. *Learning to Teach, Teaching to Learn: The Lived Experience of International Teaching Assistants at a Midwestern University* (Unpublished doctoral dissertation). Bowling Green State University, Bowling Green, OH.

Hsu, C.-F. 2012. "The Influence of Vocal Qualities and Confirmative of Nonnative English-Speaking Teachers on Student Receiver Apprehension, Affective Learning, and Cognitive Learning." *Communication Education* 61: 4–16.

Jackson, R. L., II, and K. G. Hendrix. 2003. "Racial, Cultural, and Gendered Identities in Educational Contexts: Communication Perspectives on Identity Negotiation" [Special Issue]. *Communication Education* 52: 177–317.

Kozlova, I. 2008. *Negotiation of Identities by International Teaching Assistants through the Use of Humor in University Classrooms* (Unpublished doctoral dissertation). Georgia State University, Atlanta, GA.

Li, L., J. P. Mazer, and R. Ju. 2011. "Resolving International Teaching Assistant Language Inadequacy through Dialogue: Challenges and Opportunities for Clarity and Credibility." *Communication Education* 60: 461–478.

Liu, M., D. D. Sellnow, and S. Venette. 2006. "Integrating Nonnatives as Teachers: Patterns and Perceptions of Compliance Gaining Strategies." *Communication Education* 55: 208–217.

Reed-Danahay, D., ed. 1997. *Auto/Ethnography: Rewriting the Self and the Social*. Oxford, UK: Berg Publishers.

Spry, T. 2001. "Performing Autoethnography: An Embodied Methodological Praxis." *Qualitative Inquiry* 7: 706–732.

Spry, T. 2013. "Performative Autoethnography: Critical Embodiments and Possibilities." In *Collecting and Interpreting Qualitative Materials*, edited by N. K. Denzin and Y. S. Lincoln, 4th ed., 213–244. Thousand Oaks, CA: Sage.

Trebing, D. 2007. *International Teaching Assistants' Attitudes Toward Teaching and Understanding of United States American Undergraduate Students* (Unpublished doctoral dissertation). Southern Illinois University, Carbondale, IL.

Wong (Lau), K. 2004. "Working through Identity: Understanding Class in the Context of Race, Ethnicity, and Gender." In *Our Voices: Essays in Culture, Ethnicity, and Communication*, edited by A. Gonzalez, M. Houston, and V. Chen, 256–263. Los Angeles, CA: Roxbury Press.

Yook, E. L., and R. D. Albert. 1999. "Perceptions of International Teaching Assistants: The Interrelatedness of Intercultural Training, Cognition, and Emotion." *Communication Education* 48: 1–17.

Zhang, Q., J. G. Oetzel, X. Gao, R. G. Wilcox, and J. Takai. 2007. "Teacher Immediacy Scales: Testing for Validity Across Cultures." *Communication Education* 56 (2): 228–248.

KATHERINE GRACE HENDRIX *is a professor at University of Memphis.*

APARNA HEBBANI *is a lecturer in School of Journalism & Communication, The University of Queensland.*

1

This chapter examines the negotiated experiences of a female international faculty of color teaching an intercultural communication course from the lens of intersecting cultural identities in the context of a prominently White institution in the United States.

"Are You an Immigrant?": Identity-Based Critical Reflections of Teaching Intercultural Communication

Yea-Wen Chen

Introduction

Despite blooming conversations of internationalizing higher education to meet global challenges, discussions of how international faculty experience the US academe remain scarce (for example, McCalman 2007). Yet, "the presence of international faculty members at American universities has continued to increase rapidly" (Kim, Wolf-Wendel, and Twombly 2011, 720). According to the Open Doors Report (Institute of International Education 2012), there were a total of 115,313 international scholars in the United States during the 2010–2011 year. Foote et al. (2008) even consider foreign-born academics "an invisible minority on many US campuses" (168). Although obstacles and barriers facing international faculty might run parallel to those confronting women and faculty of color, it is imperative to examine the experiences of international faculty in its own right without assuming homogeneity. For instance, Kim and colleagues (2011), based on differential experiences, propose a distinction between international faculty who earned their undergraduate degrees in their county of birth and those who received their degrees in the United States. To help shed light on the experiences of international faculty in the US academe, my chapter examines international faculty teaching through the lens of cultural identities. Specifically, I consider how international faculty's salient cultural identities inform, affect, or challenge their teaching.

There is growing recognition that the cultural identities of instructors and students "are often intertwined with what occurs in the classroom" (Cooks and Simpson 2007; McCalman 2007; Simpson, Causey, and

NEW DIRECTIONS FOR TEACHING AND LEARNING, no. 138, Summer 2014 © 2014 Wiley Periodicals, Inc.
Published online in Wiley Online Library (wileyonlinelibrary.com) • DOI: 10.1002/tl.20092

Williams 2007, 34). In particular, Manrique and Manrique (1999) found that non-European immigrant faculty emphasized the occurrences of racial prejudice and discrimination. However, little is known about how international faculty members' cultural identities affect, or become interwoven in, classroom dynamics. Informed by Brookfield's (1995) articulation of critical reflections, I unpack my experiences as a foreign-born, nonnative, non-European, and female faculty member teaching intercultural communication. In brief, Brookfield argues that reflection is important for teaching, but is not inherently critical. Reflection becomes critical when it leads "to the uncovering of paradigmatic, structuring assumptions" (8) particularly in ways that illustrate power dynamics and recognize hegemonic beliefs and practices. Guided by Brookfield's two purposes of critical reflections, I interrogate how power relations "undergird, frame, and distort educational processes and interactions" and also question assumptions and practices that work against long-term interests (8).

To illuminate the embodied negotiations of international faculty teaching, I employ a case study approach featuring ethnographically informed critical reflections on my salient cultural identities in teaching an intercultural communication course within a predominantly White institution in the United States. Consistent with both autoethnography and critical reflections, my case privileges personal narratives thereby allowing me to critically reflect on how I have come to know, experience, and/or become aware of my selfhood in teaching. In what follows, I first situate this chapter in literature on identity challenges facing international faculty and in teaching intercultural communication. Subsequently, I present my analysis of critical moments in which I experience my cultural identities affecting teaching, and conclude with pedagogical implications concerning international faculty teaching.

Brief Review of Relevant Literature

Identity negotiations are important concerns for international faculty—whether or not one is conscious of it. Questions of identity are also critical issues for the study of intercultural communication.

Identity Concerns among International Faculty.   If female faculty of color are required "to consider both their gender and race when crafting a successful professional identity" (Wright and Dinkha 2009, 107), what identity positions must international faculty consider in being, or becoming, effective teachers? There are various ways of conceptualizing the term *international faculty*, and how it is defined matters for evaluating faculty life and productivity (Kim et al. 2011). Mohanty (2011) suggests unpacking "the notion 'international faculty' by looking at it through the lens of social identity" (120); in particular, Mohanty advocates examining the ways in which international faculty respond to racialized identity positions because they are often defined by the concept of race in the US context. Similarly,

Fryberg (2010) argues that international faculty of color are subjected to "the struggler phenomenon" where junior faculty of color are perceived as "not producing enough research, and thus, as struggling to attain tenure" (186). Besides race, what other cultural identities matter in the context of international faculty teaching, and how does "international-ness" play out in the instructional context?

Currently, we know that international faculty must deal with issues of cultural identity positions (McCalman 2007; Mohanty 2011; Thomas and Johnson 2004). However, the paucity of research on international faculty tends to approach this phenomenon from a deficit model. Kim et al. (2011) evidence that most research treats international faculty as "problems, especially with respect to language and teaching skills" (742). Wright and Dinkha (2009) have synthesized the following challenges confronting female international faculty of color: (a) institutional demands for adopting professional identities that contradict personal perspectives, (b) colleagues' misinterpretations of teaching quality, and (c) students' questioning of expertise and teaching effectiveness. While it is useful to recognize identity positions that subjugate international faculty to negative stereotypes and/or everyday microinequities where minority faculty are "othered," ignored, undermined, or made to feel different or inferior (Female Science Professor 2012), a deficit model renders invisible complex and privileged identity positions (such as positions that afford social status, access to resources, or unearned favorable evaluations). To ascertain a fuller picture, I will extrapolate, interrogate, and critically reflect in this chapter cultural identity positions that both privilege and subjugate me in my being/becoming an international faculty member.

Identity Challenges in Teaching Intercultural Communication. Forces of globalization have both instigated and contributed to the growth of the study of intercultural communication. The increasing discourse of internationalization underscores the relevance of intercultural communication courses in preparing US college students to become global citizens. Yet, it remains one of the more challenging courses to teach for at least two reasons. First, the course content brings forth contestations of cultural identities within and between instructors and students (Hamlet 2009; Root et al. 2011); second, the diversifications and shifts in intercultural communication scholarship challenge the course's core objectives (DeVoss, Jasken, and Hayden 2002; Smith 1982). Whereas paradigm shifts (from functionalist perspectives to recent critical turns) in theorizing and researching intercultural communication have garnered much attention (see Halualani, Mendoza, and Drzewiecka 2009; Martin, Nakayama, and Carbaugh 2012; Rogers and Hart 2002), conversation regarding intercultural communication pedagogy, however, has remained minimal.

Given the paradigmatic "ruptures," or "junctures," in the development of intercultural communication, what implications do such ruptures have for teaching intercultural communication? Historically, the Foreign

Services Institute served as the mandate for intercultural communication training, which framed and prioritized a particular set of problems (Leeds-Hurtwitz 1990). Now, critical intercultural communication studies foreground issues of power differentials, sociohistorical contexts, and macro structures and forces in constituting and shaping intercultural communication engagements/disengagements (for example, Nakayama and Halualani 2010). In response, the continued growth of the field creates the exigency to (re)consider what teaching intercultural communication entails and what constitutes intercultural communication pedagogy. Drawing from my negotiations as a junior female international faculty of color teaching in a predominantly White institution, I (re)think the issue of cultural identities in intercultural communication pedagogy.

Critical Reflections and Analysis

Guided by Brookfield's (1995) critical reflections, I exercised self-reflexivity to analyze how my intersecting cultural identities became intertwined in teaching a large-lecture, introductory course to intercultural communication in the United States during spring 2012. I selected this course because it was my first large-lecture course with 104 students enrolled across majors and also my first time working with a teaching associate. As the US higher education is witnessing an ever-increasing number of large-lecture classes especially in public universities, this case serves not just to further intercultural communication pedagogy but also to examine identity-based issues in large-lecture formats. To prompt critical reflections of my intersecting cultural identities, I relied on collaborative teaching reflections between my teaching associate and me. In particular, I attended to the ways in which power relations and unquestioned assumptions and practices undergirded how I experienced myself as an international faculty in class.

Case Background.   The selected course took place within a predominantly White institution in the Midwestern United States. According to its Office of Institutional Research, in fall 2010, there were 17,404 (81.6 percent) White students followed by 1,491 (7.0 percent) internationals, 958 (4.5 percent) African Americans, 504 (2.4 percent) Hispanics, 382 (1.8 percent) two or more races, 212 (1.0 percent) Asian Americans, 61 (0.3 percent) Native Americans, and 24 (0.1 percent) Hawaiians/Pacific Islanders. Within my intercultural communication course, the majority of students were White, middle-class individuals between the ages of 18–24 from major cities in Ohio. I, a transnational Asian woman, was the principal instructor, and Nathanial Simmons, a White male from Oklahoma, served as the teaching associate. Mirroring an apprenticeship system, assisting professors was one way for graduate students in my department to become eligible to teach the introductory intercultural communication course. As part of a larger study that aims to unpack the challenges and opportunities embedded in teaching and learning about cultural identities, Nathaniel and

I blogged, via a WordPress site, about any critical, or memorable, moments following each class session. As an example, on April 23, 2012, one of the issues that we blogged about was a surprising interaction where a White male student openly questioned if I was an immigrant. Nathaniel wrote, " ... he [the White, male student] asked 'Are you an immigrant?' ... You asked, 'You haven't been listening, have you?' Personally, I was shocked. On numerous occasions you have mentioned that you are from Taiwan and have even mentioned the process of obtaining permanent residency." I commented, "Though I initially said that I was not bothered by the open questioning of my immigration status, I am still thinking and wondering how I really feel about it." I utilized these blog exchanges as materials for conducting my critical reflections.

Pedagogically, my approach to teaching intercultural communication largely reflected and was informed by Fassett and Warren's (2007) critical communication pedagogy that views culture as central, conceives identity as constituted in communication, approaches power as fluid and complex, and focuses on illuminating "concrete, mundane communication practices as constitutive of larger social structural systems" (43). Prior to this course, I wrestled with how to reconcile my own theoretical lens in teaching intercultural communication from diverse theoretical perspectives (for example, functionalist, interpretive, and critical). Eventually, I settled with a decidedly critical approach to teaching intercultural communication, viewing education as transformative, and grounded in social/global justice.

To contextualize my intersecting cultural identities, I should first describe my salient cultural identities/identifications. As a transnational women originally from Taiwan, I embarked on my sojourn in the United States in 2004. I use the term "transnational" to signify that my experiences transcend traditional notions of nation state; that is, I am not *just* Taiwanese, American, nor the cumulative sum of both nationalities. Growing up as a "Han-Chinese" in a predominantly Taiwanese-speaking household, I acquired multilingual awareness early on to differentiate groups of people based on their spoken languages (for example, Taiwanese, Mandarin Chinese, and Hakka). I was raised in a large, traditional, three-generation, working-class family. At a young age, I became aware of various ways in which difference mattered (for example, sex and gender, socioeconomic status, and so on). It was not until I came to the United States that I experienced being racialized as Asian on a daily basis and reexamined my relationship with globalization and the choices that I had made such as pursuing my postgraduate degrees in the United States.

Moments of Becoming (Re)Racialized as a Minority Faculty. One of the core learning objectives of my intercultural communication course was for students to become aware and reflective of the cultural positions from which they experienced their social worlds. As a racialized Asian woman in a predominantly White institution, race and racism—directly or indirectly—were examples that I frequently chose for in-class discussions and applications. I kicked off the course with the controversial Trayvon Martin case[1] (the fatal shooting of a Black teenager in Florida in February 2012) to demonstrate the importance and material consequences of intercultural/interracial communication in everyday practices. Later, I employed *Mooz-lum*—an independent film directed by Qasim "Q" Basir (2011) about the identity struggles of a (Black) Muslim male to redefine his selfhood in the United States—as a case to discuss perceptual problematics in intercultural communication (for example, prejudices, stereotypes, attribution errors, and so on). As exemplified here, I often selected US-based cases that were familiar and relatable to the students and anchored on the US race politics as a starting point for framing and building on discussions. By doing so, I positioned myself as Asian and forced both my students and me to confront in class how we were woven into the US racial fabrics and cultural politics. Further, whenever discussing race as a social construction with no fixed meanings, I allowed my race to be complexly read or interpreted by different students (for example, Asian [American], East Asian, Taiwanese, and so on). Thus, I found myself constantly negotiating feeling (re)racialized in moments of discussing race and awkwardly questioning what my "Asian-ness" meant.

One of the ways in which I experienced my (re)racialization—the processes of (re)creating races and (re)constituting racial meanings—was in moments of awkwardness and/or resistance. On April 16, 2012, Nathaniel watched *Mooz-lum* for the first time in class, blogged about the film afterward, and wrote: "For teaching purposes I think it is 'hitting' where many of our students are. Many have left home, some for the first time, and are 'going away from' or 'rethinking' their belief structures." I, on the other hand, felt awkward sitting in class that day, especially when some students started to get up and leave without viewing the film in its entirety. My initial awkwardness resulted from concerns with how the students might perceive the film. To what extent might the early departure suggest resistance to the film, the class, or me? Did my message come across as intended— a call for critical awareness of how race remains an important yet invisible lens of perceiving the self and others? Did *Mooz-lum* actually *expose* or *perpetuate* problematic stereotypes about (Black) Muslims? The worksheet responses confirmed some of my concerns; for example, many students indicated that they couldn't identify with the protagonist, a college-age Black Muslim male.

Another aspect of my awkwardness centered on classroom management. The large-lecture setting afforded a certain level of anonymity. Unlike my smaller classes, it was not possible to establish a comparable level of immediacy to ameliorate the discomfort associated with discussing difficult topics, such as racism. Further, my awkwardness was complicated by problematic representations of non-Muslim Blacks in this film, of which I was not acutely aware until sitting in the presence of my students across races. On the worksheet, a minority student picked up on this and wrote,

"It seems that one of the only Black kids in the room was portrayed as being loud. This portrayal falsely reflects the African American community." That day, I felt challenged and unsure of my racial positionality. In instances like *Mooz-lum* where race was constructed as a Black–White problem with no other racial groups represented, how had my students related to me, and how should I have situated myself as a racial other?

The debriefing of *Mooz-lum* the next class was met with great resistance that both Nathaniel and I noted. Nathaniel commented, "I was surprised by the worksheet 'resistance' that we encountered. Students were very slow and appeared to not want to speak in groups within this mass lecture class. Why do you think this is?" Similarly, I reflected,

> In the process of debriefing the film *Mooz-lum* (2011), I felt and sensed certain tension and resistance to become engaged. Are most of the students already tired of discussing race-based issues? Have the discussions so far exhausted all the factors and forces in considering race relations (in the United States)? I don't think so.

Unlike discussions of the Trayvon Martin case that left little room for denying the relevance of race in this "postracial" society, *Mooz-lum* was complexly anchored on the intersections between race, gender, Islam, and/or Islamophobia in a post-9/11 climate. Originally, I thought my students could relate to the college setting in *Mooz-lum*, but I did not foresee the additional layers of complexities associated with storytelling from the perspective of a Black and Muslim male. Was it too uncomfortable to witness Whites being portrayed as perpetrators in a film that touched upon 9/11? Did it seem a peculiar choice for me as a non-Muslim, non-Black, and Asian female to show this film in class? Further, a myriad of other factors might have contributed to the student resistance including: mass lecture effect where students did not feel safe in speaking up especially about race, foreignness effect where the students did not find the film *Mooz-lum* relatable or relevant, and mid-quarter effect where the newness, if not exoticness, of this course slowly wore off.

This incident exemplified the negotiated moments of awkwardness and resistance for me, as a racialized Asian faculty, to facilitate discussions of race in my intercultural communication course. While the film *Mooz-lum* created spaces for examining and discussing racial prejudices and stereotypes within the context of US racial terrains, it also reminded me of how little I knew about the historical and political struggles of (Black) Muslims, which contributed to my awkwardness, equivocality, and uncertainty as a racialized other. It was a worthwhile exercise, but I didn't feel as effective as I could have been with a different example in which I could resort and tap into my salient cultural identities as resources.

Critically processing this activity made me aware of several ways in which my negotiated racial position(s) became intertwined with my

NEW DIRECTIONS FOR TEACHING AND LEARNING • DOI: 10.1002/tl

teaching. First, when teaching intercultural communication in a predominantly White institution in the Midwestern United States, I found my racial identity most salient as I frequently employed US-based race examples. In doing so, my sense of self became constituted vis-à-vis the examples that I chose and I became (re)racialized in the processes of discussing, negotiating, and unpacking race relations implicated in the examples. That is, I experienced my Asian-ness differently across the examples and conversations in class. Second, I experienced myself not just as Asian, but also as an Asian immigrant, a heterosexual East Asian, an Asian/Taiwanese woman, and so on. For example, I was decidedly Asian when my students laughed out loud at my self-deprecation as "a bad Asian driver." However, I turned into an Asian immigrant when my students and I discussed US regional differences between "pop" and "soda," of which I had no definite understanding. My Asian-ness was fluid and evasive as it became interlinked with my Taiwan-ness/Chinese-ness, foreignness, gender, class, and so on, which informed my teaching of cultural identities. Third, processing this activity made me more acutely aware of how much weight I placed on addressing racism in an intercultural communication course and if I might consider diversifying and addressing other "-isms" as well.

Moments of "Othered" as a Foreign Faculty. Consistent with Mohanty's (2011) argument, I responded to and negotiated my racial identity position. However, there were other moments where I was defined more by my status as a foreign faculty than my race. As a transnational woman, my international-ness came across in several ways. First, my international-ness was reflected in the shared-unshared cultural knowledge, memory, and experience. For example, when discussing how histories influenced intercultural communication, I shared the contested meanings that surrounded Chairman Mao. Nathaniel observed and reminded me that this Chinese icon was unfamiliar to our students. He wrote, "I wonder how many people know who Chairman Mao from China is. Perhaps next time this example is used it would be beneficial to have a photograph and to briefly state who Chairman Mao is." As much as I could briefly explain Chairman Mao, it would be difficult for me to describe the cultural intimacy surrounding this Chinese political icon to my American students. Thus, my foreignness was marked by the odd gaps of unshared cultural intimacy, which required amending, bridging, and negotiating.

Secondly, the subject of intercultural communication both legitimized and perpetuated my foreignness. On the one hand, my experiences growing up in Taiwan and my struggles as a cultural other became relevant materials in this course; on the other hand, I feared becoming the "token" international faculty, or a "prototypical" Taiwanese woman, where students interpreted what I did or said as representative of my cultural groups. Yet, as a critical intercultural communication scholar, I also experienced more opportunities in this course for demystifying, exposing, or problematizing take-for-granted assumptions about "international faculty." For example, since English language competence is discussed as a common problem among international faculty (for example, Kim et al. 2011), I battled my students' perceiving me as having a foreign accent or difficult to comprehend since day one of entering the classroom, and decided to confront this issue. When discussing whether or not to take a course from an international instructor, some of my students admitted feeling apprehensive about signing up for my class when they initially saw my foreign last name and others protested having to take a course from a foreign instructor whom they struggled to understand. Then, one White female remarked that she found me more understandable than one of her US American professors from a different region of the United States, which shifted and deepened the discussion to complicate the notion of "foreign" faculty. While I cherished such a learning moment, I was also cognizant that to some students, I would remain too foreign to approach, understand, or listen to.

Lastly, when unpacking my identities as an international faculty member, I recognized that my international-ness was simultaneously raced, classed, and gendered. However, when examining my teaching reflections, I noticed that I was most aware of my race and my foreignness and, in comparison, less aware of my gender except for an interaction where a male student challenged one of his assignment grades and I was glad to have Nathaniel present. I had met with this student early on because he struggled with learning about how differences (for example, race, class, and so on) still mattered in my course whereas he fundamentally believed that equalities had been achieved. Though I had been aware of his defensiveness toward this course, I was still surprised by his public display of his dismay for a grade that he just received. I first tried to speak with him in private, but he could not really listen to me in that moment. Since Nathaniel had graded his paper, I decided to involve him next and let him explain the grading criteria to the student. And it was the right move to involve the White male authority figure.

In terms of socioeconomic status, my working-class background was important to me but it had less impact on my teaching. As a working-class intellectual, I experienced class stratifications firsthand, but I seldom focused on it in this course. Compared with race, class seemed less salient or targeted to me in this course. It could also be that I didn't feel equipped with necessary vernacular to effectively discuss class issues. Or maybe because my class positionality had shifted those experiences were less immediate and personal in my current position. Nonetheless, I was not just an international faculty member, but a heterosexual, transnational female faculty of color originally from Taiwan.

Conclusion

Relying on ethnographically informed teaching reflections, I examined in this chapter moments of my negotiations as a female international faculty of color in an intercultural communication course at a predominantly White university in the United States. Specifically, I unpacked memorable moments of becoming aware of my salient identities in class and how those moments of critical awareness informed and affected my teaching. Overall, my Asian-ness and foreignness emerged as most salient, contested, and fluid as intertwined with course materials that I had chosen, and to some extent intersect with my gender and class. Those negotiated moments of being (re)racialized and becoming "othered" are highly contingent on the in-class conversations and interactions, which underscore the contextualized nature of identity negotiations. Also, in negotiating my selfhood in class, my targeted cultural identities did not just subjugate me to stereotypes but also served as resources for deepening my engagement with my students. Thus, my findings underscore the need for (non-European) international faculty to respond to racialized identity positions and address racial prejudice and discrimination (Manrique and Manrique 1999; Mohanty 2011). Additionally, this chapter demonstrates the utility of applying critical reflections to better understand the negotiations of international faculty from the lens of salient cultural identities.

Given both the similarities and differences between my students and me, I continue to struggle at cultivating a learning climate where the students feel supported yet challenged to address difficult issues, such as racism. As introductory courses in public universities continue to increase in size, the challenges that I have faced are now amplified in large-lecture courses where an international faculty member can seem all the more foreign. However, these challenges can become productive spaces for deconstructing power relations through critical reflections and can turn into transformative spaces given appropriate institutional support and mentorship. Considering the heterogeneity between and among intercultural faculty, I want to caution that my experiences should not be taken or interpreted out of context. Finally, I urge that the increased internationalization of higher education demand more attention to the experiences of international faculty members across divergent identity positions.

Note

1. The fatal shooting of Trayvon Martin, a 17-year-old Black teenager, inside a gated community in Florida aroused attentions and controversies from communities across the United States. On the night of February 26, 2012, George Zimmerman, a multiracial Hispanic male, spotted Martin walking inside the community where Zimmerman was a neighborhood watch coordinator and reported his behavior as "suspicious" to the police. The incident led to a violent encounter where Zimmerman fatally shot unarmed Martin.

References

Basir, Q. 2011. *Mooz-lum*. United States: Peace Film.
Brookfield, S. D. 1995. *Becoming a Critically Reflective Teacher*. San Francisco, CA: Jossey-Bass.

Cooks, L. M., and J. Simpson, eds. 2007. *Whiteness, Pedagogy, Performance: Dis/placing Race*. Lanham, MD: Lexington Books.

DeVoss, D., J. Jasken, and D. Hayden. 2002. "Teaching Intracultural and Intercultural Communication: A Critique and Suggested Method." *Journal of Business and Technical Communication* 16: 69–94.

Fassett, D. L., and J. T. Warren. 2007. *Critical Communication Pedagogy*. Thousand Oaks, CA: Sage.

Female Science Professor [pseud.]. 2012, August 5. "Dear Sir" [Electronic Version]. *The Chronicle of Higher Education*. Accessed August 14, 2012. http://chronicle.com/article/Dear-Sir/133283/.

Foote, K. E., W. Li, J. Monk, and R. Theobald. 2008. "Symposium: Foreign-Born Scholars in US Universities: Issues, Concerns, and Strategies." *Journal of Geography in Higher Education* 32 (2): 167–178.

Fryberg, S. A. 2010. "Constructing Junior Faculty of Color as Strugglers: The Implications for Tenure and Promotion." In *The Future of Diversity: Academic Leaders Reflect on American Higher Education*, edited by D. Little and S. P. Mohanty, 181–217. New York, NY: Palgrave Macmillan.

Halualani, R. T., S. L. Mendoza, and J. A. Drzewiecka. 2009. "'Critical' Junctures in Intercultural Communication Studies: A Review." *The Review of Communication* 9 (1): 17–35.

Hamlet, J. D. 2009. "Engaging Spirituality and An Authentic Self in the Intercultural Communication Class." In *As the Spirit Moves Us: Embracing Spirituality in the Postsecondary Experience*, New Directions for Teaching and Learning, no. 120, edited by K. G. Hendrix and J. D. Hamlet, 25–33. San Francisco, CA: Jossey-Bass.

Institute of International Education. 2012. *Open Doors Data: International Scholars: All Places of Origin*. Accessed August 12, 2012. http://www.iie.org/Research-and-Publications/Open-Doors/Data/International-Scholars/All-Places-of-Origin/2009-11.

Kim, D., L. Wolf-Wendel, and S. Twombly. 2011. "International Faculty: Experiences of Academic Life and Productivity in U.S. Universities." *The Journal of Higher Education* 82 (6): 720–747.

Leeds-Hurtwitz, W. 1990. "Notes in the History of Intercultural Communication: The Foreign Service Institute and the Mandate for Intercultural Training." *Quarterly Journal of Speech* 76: 262–281.

Manrique, C. G., and G. G. Manrique. 1999. *The Multicultural or Immigrant Faculty in American Society*. Lewiston, NY: Edwin Mellen Press.

Martin, J. N., T. K. Nakayama, and D. Carbaugh. 2012. "The History and Development of the Study of Intercultural Communication and Applied Linguistics." In *The Routledge Handbook of Language and Intercultural Communication*, edited by J. Jackson, 17–36. New York, NY: Routledge.

McCalman, C. L. 2007. "Being an Intercultural Competent Instructor in the United States: Issues of Classroom Dynamics and Appropriateness, and Recommendations for International Instructors." In *Neither White Nor Male: Female Faculty of Color*, New Directions for Teaching and Learning, no. 110, edited by K. G. Hendrix, 65–74. San Francisco, CA: Jossey-Bass.

Mohanty, S. P. 2011. "Race, Identity, and International Faculty on US Campuses." In *Bridging Cultures: International Women Faculty Transforming the US Academy*, edited by S. R. Robbins, S. H. Smith, and F. Santini, 117–122. Lanham, MD: University Press of America.

Nakayama, T. K., and R. T. Halualani, eds. 2010. *The Handbook of Critical Intercultural Communication*. Oxford, UK: Wiley-Blackwell.

Rogers, E. M., and W. B. Hart. 2002. "The Histories of Intercultural, International, and Development Communication." In *Handbook of International and Intercultural*

Communication, edited by W. B. Gudykunst and B. Mody, 2nd ed., 1–18. Thousand Oaks, CA: Sage.

Root, E., T. D. Hardgrove, M. D. Petrunia, and A. Ngampornchai. 2011, November. "The Voice at the Front of the Room: Identity Dialectics of the Intercultural Communication Instructor." Paper presented at the Annual Conference of the National Communication Association, New Orleans, LA.

Simpson, J. S., A. Causey, and L. Williams. 2007. "'I Would Want You to Understand It': Students' Perceptions on Addressing Race in the Classroom." *Journal of Intercultural Communication Research* 36 (1): 33–50.

Smith, A. G. 1982. "Content Decisions in Intercultural Communication." *The Southern Speech Communication Journal* 47: 252–262.

Thomas, J. M., and B. J. Johnson. 2004. "Perspectives of International Faculty Members: Their Experiences and Stories." *Education and Society* 22 (3): 47–64.

Wright, S., and J. Dinkha. 2009. "Gendered Reality, Professional Identity, and Women of Color in Higher Education." In *When "Minorities Are Strongly Encouraged to Apply,"* edited by D. Cleveland, 103–118. New York, NY: Peter Lang.

YEA-WEN CHEN is an assistant professor in the School of Communication Studies at Ohio University.

2

In the post 9/11 world, a nonnative US teacher who attempts to challenge existing cultural assumptions may easily trigger hostility and suspicion in the classroom. This chapter conveys the experience of a college professor whose approach often deliberately crosses that line.

College Is Not a Restaurant: Challenging Cultural Hegemony in the US Classroom

Juraj Kittler

Introduction

The earliest iterations of the *standpoint theory* were formulated by a group of feminist scholars who were looking at the world mainly through the prism of gender and race (Harding and Hintikka 1983). Consequently, they claimed that all knowledge was socially located and shaped by cultural assumptions. To position myself properly in the context of this autoethnographic chapter, I must disclose that I am neither a woman nor a person of color. Yet I am not a traditional White Anglo-Saxon Protestant either.

I was born in the mid-1960s in Czechoslovakia (today's Slovakia), a country that was for centuries under the spell of the Austro-Hungarian Empire. In the post-WWII era, Czechoslovakia was politically dominated by the Communist Party (until 1989). Consequently, I completed my master's degree within a social system that was diametrically different from the conditions in a "typical" private liberal arts college of the northeastern United States where I currently teach. Indeed, most of the observations contained in this study reflect encounters between such diverse academic cultures—one in which I grew up and the other in which I currently work. Even after ten continuous years spent in US classrooms at three different campuses, I am still struggling to collate myself and my academic identity between those two cultures, continuously juggling between their often contradictory epistemic influences on my life.

This chapter is dedicated to my dissertation adviser, Dr. Ronald V. Bettig.

NEW DIRECTIONS FOR TEACHING AND LEARNING, no. 138, Summer 2014 © 2014 Wiley Periodicals, Inc.
Published online in Wiley Online Library (wileyonlinelibrary.com) • DOI: 10.1002/tl.20093

While initially praised for its innovative approach, *standpoint theory* with its notion of the situated nature of knowledge was soon under attack by those who pointed out its essentialist assumptions that attributed all determining power to social structure, leaving almost no space for individual human agency. Among the approaches that may help the researcher offset this handicap was the *positioning theory* developed in the 1990s by social psychologists who previously relied on static concepts such as social role or standpoint (Davies and Harré 1990; Harré and Van Langenhove 1999). The idea of positioning was adopted as the theoretical framework for my study because it conceptualizes the epistemological *position* of the observer as dialectic interplay between nature and nurture, structure and agency, by adding to the original concept of *standpoint* (reflecting only the cultural norms of a particular reference group) the predispositions and experiences unique to each individual. Positioning theory claims that the resulting complex sociopsychological *positions* are reflected in verbal and nonverbal speech acts in which the individual subjectivities are produced and reproduced through a set of empirically observable discursive practices.

Furthermore, the concepts of *position* and *positioning* dovetail nearly perfectly with the autoethnographic observation that informs the methodological aspect of my work. Ellis and Bochner (2000) define the autoethnographic approach as a way to tease out multiple layers of consciousness, while the scholar aims at reconciling his or her unique personal psychological experience with the cultural phenomena that informed it. These authors expected researchers to constantly look back and forth, "first through an ethnographic wide-angle lens, focusing outward on social and cultural aspects of the personal experience; then they look inward, exposing a vulnerable self that is moved by and may move through, refract and resist cultural interpretations" (739).

I found the autoethnographic approach and its ability to capture the subjective intrapsychic processes triggered by intercultural encounters almost perfectly suited to convey my own experience as a nonnative English speaker in the American classroom. Ellis (2004) claimed that the resulting autoethnographic observation stemmed from "the interplay of the introspective, personally engaged self with cultural descriptions mediated through language, history, and ethnographic explanation" (38). Indeed, history and histories—both individual and collective—are an important aspect of any ethnographic observation. As a communication historian, I don't need to be reminded of that. Thus, at the point when I am getting ready to plunge into the analysis of my own subjective experience in the contemporary American classroom, my mind inadvertently recalls some interesting nineteenth century observations of the US educational system that I stumbled upon while working on my own research; beyond any doubt, they deeply influenced my own understanding of the issue.

Historical European Attitudes toward the US Education System?

In the 1830s and 1840s, European intellectuals increasingly began to pay attention to American progress. Famous social observers of various nationalities, each under different circumstances and on separate occasions, visited the United States in order to study the constitutional system and social institutions of the new republic which so much excited the European political imagination.[1] Because of the quality of their observations, most of them can be doubtlessly considered early sociologists—although some of their remarks must appear naïve to today's reader—while others were driven by cultural prejudices that the Old World continued to hold against the New. However, I noticed that those authors who addressed the state of US education in their memoirs struck an almost unanimous chord: in comparison to European schooling, the American mind was, in their eyes, significantly more practically oriented—it valued almost exclusively only those forms of knowledge that could have an immediate tangible use.

"The people have no objection to a clever surgeon or learned physician, because they profit by their skill. An ingenious mechanic they respect. There is a fair field for a chemist or engineer," wrote one of the most outspoken foreign critiques, Scottish traveler and author Thomas Hamilton (1834, 365). But, he added, the people whom he met during his US journey did not value any forms of knowledge that would not have implied an immediate practical benefit. "In short, the state of American society is such as to afford no leisure for any thing [sic] so unmarketable as abstract knowledge" (364). Hamilton's famous contemporary, Alexis de Tocqueville (1898), seconded the claim by pointing out that even science is "taken up as a matter of business, and the only branch of it which is attended to is such as admits of an immediate practical application" (53). Tocqueville's compatriot Michel Chevalier (1839) argued that in order to educate a Frenchmen, an elaborate curriculum based on general principles is first required in order to "metamorphose all his thoughts and habits," while the American "learns by example merely" (347–348).

Landing on the US coast almost two centuries later, and shortly after embarking on a career as a college instructor, I similarly struggled to make sense of the US system of higher education that was to become my professional home for some time to come. Frankly, it was the collection of writings of the early European observers that helped me crystallize some of my own thoughts. I realized that they, just like me now, struggled with the same principal issues: the level of commodification of higher education in the United States that exceeded anything ever seen in Europe, with the consequent tendency to foster practically oriented forms of knowledge at the expense of abstract philosophical concepts. Not one day passes in my teaching life where I don't inadvertently stumble upon a situation that

NEW DIRECTIONS FOR TEACHING AND LEARNING • DOI: 10.1002/tl

reminds me of the continuous salience of such issues, and I would like to share some of this experience with you, the reader.

Personal Experience with the Aversion to Abstract Forms of Knowledge

My first US academic appointment was to teach media and journalism at one of the satellite campuses of a big state university. I am a former editor with an extensive track record in both print and radio. Reflecting on my own educational experience back in Europe, I started my first 300-level Magazine Editing class with a brief excursion down the lines of the industry's history. I covered the gradual evolution of both magazine content and its design, addressed different types and structures of magazine articles, touched upon the dramaturgic composition of an issue, and did a brief review of different graphic elements in regard to the overall legibility—when my students suddenly revolted. One morning, they did not show up for class; instead, they organized their own spite-seminar in the library.

The whole affair ended up in the department chair's office. "Why is he pushing us through all this nonsense that has *nothing* to do with magazine editing?" argued Stacy, the most outspoken of the rebels. I barely understood what she was talking about. It was an upper division course that, in my opinion, naturally called for some historical and philosophical depth. "Look, most of those kids will end up working for some state agency or private company where they may be put in charge of a weekly or monthly newsletter. Why all that fuss? Just show them how to put together a four-page bulletin and they will all be happy as clams," my colleague Peter said, trying to calm down the situation.

I remember coming home from that meeting in a state of devastation, sitting mindlessly in our living room when I inadvertently opened one of the locally published magazines lying on our coffee table and started paging through it. Suddenly, something caught my interest and I began paying more attention to the content. Overall, the editorial materials were just fillers to justify the amount of advertisements that seemed to be the real *raison d'être* of this publication. Most of the pieces I surveyed lacked any conceptual framework and the attention to detail in their layout was almost nonexistent. Soon I realized that it was a perfect showcase of all the *don'ts* that I was trying to communicate, in vain, to my "practically oriented" students. I skimmed another three to four locally produced consumer magazines lying on our table and they all suffered from the same flaws. This sudden glimpse into US journalistic practices made me understand that I was expecting my students—who had minimal experience with professionally edited publications like *Time* or *Newsweek*—to do something that was countercultural, to say the least.

Currently, I teach at a liberal arts college that is, by definition, more open to the pursuit of abstract forms of knowledge. Yet, the economic crisis

NEW DIRECTIONS FOR TEACHING AND LEARNING • DOI: 10.1002/tl

of 2008 that took away a significant portion of my university's endowment opened up a new round of debates between those who arduously defend the traditional liberal arts model and those who were trying to link each department to a concrete profession corresponding mainly with lucrative positions in the job market. As I write this chapter, my university is discussing the addition of a new business major, which sets some of my colleagues on edge. Increasingly valued are mainly those curricula that can produce alumni who can later help the school grow its endowment.

While it is true that there are still some small and for the most part also thriving islands in the US college universe where abstract knowledge is cherished and cultivated, it is also true that their shores are gradually being eroded. This is due not only to the state of the economy in the aftermath of the 2008 financial crisis but also because of the increasing measure to which the "practically oriented" neoliberal ideology influences the spirit of American academia (compare Ball 2012; Bok 2004).

A College or a Restaurant?   In the first three or four years of my US classroom experience I learned a lot from those whom I was supposed to teach. Previously, I had spent three years of teaching as a graduate student back in Czechoslovakia, a country that historically inherited the Austrian-German model of education, which was later infused with a substantial dosage of Soviet influence. In any case, at the core of both pedagogical templates was the idea of a "Herr Teacher"—an absolute authority in the classroom whom everybody respected out of a combination of reverence and fear.

"Professor, you came from a different country and you may not understand that here in America we pay a lot for our education," argued one of my students halfway through the third semester of my US college journey when I asked the class to write informal feedback on my pedagogy. "Just imagine that you go to a restaurant, pay for your meal and the waiter would stand over you, telling you to eat faster or to finish your veggies," he wrote and added: "How would you feel?"

I first wanted to dismiss the comment as pure nonsense—maybe an anecdote that I can tell back in Europe to my friends in order to illustrate the gloomy state of US college education. But something inside was telling me that if this is actually how some of my students felt, I had better pay more attention to their complaints. Next time in class, I asked the student for his permission to read the comment out loud. After doing so, I carefully weighed each word and said something like: "I understand that you have to pay for your education. Indeed, I grew up in a system where I got mine for free. Instead of accumulating student loans, the government was actually paying us for studying in the form of scholarships for good grades." I paused to let the words sink, took a deep breath, and challenged the comparison between the college and the restaurant. Instead, I offered another, very different parallel. "Imagine you go to see your dentist," I told the class. "A doctor's time is much more expensive than mine. Yet, in order for the

NEW DIRECTIONS FOR TEACHING AND LEARNING • DOI: 10.1002/tl

dentist to deliver a contracted service, he or she must inevitably cause you some pain..." I am not sure whether the comparison of education with drilling teeth was the best, but it worked with my students by helping them understand that some things simply cannot be achieved without some sacrifice that may be even painful at times.

The Student Perceived as Our Client.   Several years ago, *The New York Times* published an article by Greg Winter (2003) entitled quite tellingly "Jacuzzi U.? A Battle of Perks to Lure Students." It was about the skyrocketing cost of US higher education, paradoxically driven by services and facilities that are not essential to the educational process. Yet my students came to expect such perks without realizing that it is they who will be stuck with the bill.

Sometimes, I watch groups of our potential students when they come with parents to explore the campus. They rarely ask questions about the quality of our math department or our library collections. Understandably, they want to see the gym, student center, dining room, and dorms. And the university that must compete for their attention with other peer institutions gives them what they want. With the economic downturn in 2008, when the endowment of my school plummeted, every dollar of tuition that can help us stay in the black counts. The reign of the bottom line is omnipresent. I noticed that not only our administrators but also some professors from time to time address students as "our clients" when discussing academic issues during our faculty meetings. Such an attitude is being inadvertently, but steadily ingrained in our institutional culture.

And our students are well aware of such dynamics. I had a young woman—I will call her Anne—who was apparently one of the full tuition paying students enrolled in one of my journalism classes. I previously had some unpleasant experiences with plagiarism in this course, so I constantly reminded students that all quotations they use in their articles must be honestly obtained through personal or telephone interviews. Anne filed two stories that piqued my curiosity simply because the quotes she used were too polished for a beginner. I randomly "Googled" some of them and found three that were copied verbatim from the Internet, among others, from a CNN website.

After an unsuccessful attempt to settle the issue within class, I filed a case with the Academic Honor Council. My suspicion was confirmed; Anne challenged the decision and lost. As for me, the story ended right there. But not for Anne and her parents. Unbeknown to me, it triggered a flurry of correspondence with my supervisors, and in the end, her parents personally visited the campus. To make a long story short, Anne transferred to another university and her father wrote an angry farewell letter that he sent to all of my supervisors in which he called me a "bully" and added that while "education cannot be measured in dollars and cents, for $50,000 per year" Anne's family "expected better."

NEW DIRECTIONS FOR TEACHING AND LEARNING • DOI: 10.1002/tl

It is to the credit of my institution that it stood behind me and upheld the plagiarism verdict. Yet, during the whole process, nobody gave me the opportunity to explain my side of the story. The university managed the case as a PR issue, trying first to avert the loss of a "client," and after that failed, to minimize the damage to its institutional image. At least from my perspective, Anne perceived the whole affair as an angry restaurant client that was stuck with an expensive bill for a meal that wasn't as fun to consume as she was promised during the recruitment process, whereas from her perspective she probably felt that she received the short end of the stick.

Are You a Communist?   While working on my PhD and teaching a class at a large US state university, I taught a first-generation college student whom I particularly liked because of his sincere struggle with the course assignments despite not-so-stellar results. Bill had a full-time job and often showed up at our morning class right after his night shift. He approached me once right after class and said almost ashamedly: "Professor, would you mind if I ask you something?" I nodded, and after brief hesitation he finally got it out: "Are you a Communist?"

I remained speechless. When they came to power in my native Czechoslovakia in 1948, the Communists confiscated a great deal of my family's property, despite the fact that we were only moderately wealthy. I was reminded of it every time we talked politics at the dinner table, which was indeed one of the most common topics of our family conversations. My father listened every night to one of the subversive anti-Communist broadcasts financed by the US Congress, which often upset my mother. "Are you crazy? What if the neighbors overhear you, just think of the kids," she would often reproach him. Never mind, I joined Dad in listening when I was about twelve, and this illegal conspiracy became our most favorite pastime.

During the wave of anti-Communist uprisings that swept Eastern Europe in 1989, I was in grad school and naturally became one of the leading voices at my university among those who were against the regime, which—I was informed later—earned me one of the top spots on the list that our Communist dean prepared for the secret police. All this, only to be suspected now by Bill of being a Communist myself?

"Why do you think I should be a Communist?" I asked Bill, sincerely puzzled, but also amused by such an unexpected accusation. "Because you have that funny Eastern European accent, very much like a Russian," he argued, "and you sometimes talk about strange stuff that sounds quite un-American to me." I was trying to recollect our most recent class discussions. Oh, indeed, we covered one of my favorite topics: the public broadcasting system as an alternative to the private business model. As usual, I used the example of the British BBC when trying to explain to students the full potential of broadcasting relying on public funding. I mentioned it to Bill and he nodded. "But why do you think that BBC has something to do with Communism?" I asked. "Well, it certainly doesn't promote our values of the free market," he answered without too much hesitation. I saw in Bill's face that for him, this constituted clear proof of my ideological positions that were questionable to say the least, and he was now struggling to wrap his mind around the fact that he just exposed what he thought was my true identity.

A Nonnative Teacher Challenging US Hegemony

As a communication historian whose work is influenced by political economy and critical-cultural scholarship, I very well understand how explosive the material that I teach can be. My US dissertation adviser would often tell me that some of the kids in his classes were, for the first time in their lives, exposed to readings challenging the hegemonic tenets upon which US society traditionally operated. "I have one single crack at getting them to think outside the box, and damned if I let that opportunity escape," Ron used to say. "For their own sake, to show them that there are different worlds outside of their own."

But the private liberal arts university where I teach now has been traditionally recruiting its students among the upper and upper-middle classes that often owe their fortunes to Madison Avenue, K Street, or Wall Street. Every time I teach a class focusing on media and public communication, I become extremely aware that I have in front of me students whose parents may work for the industries that I critically scrutinize in my lectures.

Zinn (2000) once argued that a classroom creates a unique situation in which "an adult, looked upon as a mentor, is alone with a group of young people for a protracted and officially sanctioned period of time and can assign whatever reading he or she chooses and discuss with these young people, any subject under the sun" (173). I am quite aware that the very selection of readings is an expression of a teacher's political position. Yet Zinn emphasized that despite the instructor's own ideology, s/he must always leave space for an opposing view expressed by students "and scrupulously uphold their right to disagree with me" (175).

And yet, this is not an easy task for a nonnative teacher like me. Although I now have US citizenship and I "look" just like most of my students (that is, Anglo in appearance), my nonnative roots are revealed every time I open my mouth. After the above-mentioned experience with Bill, I am always very cautious of how much I can "rock the boat" when challenging my students' social and cultural assumptions. I developed a habit of reminding them several times during the semester that it is indeed my goal to make them feel uneasy about the world they have been living in ever since their birth. "If you feel that I am trying to pull the rug out from under you, if you become upset at least time to time during semester because of our readings and discussions, it means that I am doing my job," I emphasize. But not all remember my warning and such students never forget to point out in their end-of-the-year evaluations that the wacko teacher tried to push some strange ideas on them.

NEW DIRECTIONS FOR TEACHING AND LEARNING • DOI: 10.1002/tl

Pitting Children against Their Own Parents?

My colleagues—whose teaching is similarly informed by the critical-cultural approach—sometimes jokingly remark that our classes may be turning some of our affluent students against their own fathers (and of course, entrepreneurial mothers, too). But occasionally, this may become more than just an innocent joke. Some years ago, I had a senior student in my class—let's call him Henry—whose family was closely tied to a prestigious PR and advertising firm. As far as I understood the situation, Henry's tuition was basically paid for from an account set aside by his grandmother who founded the company. He was enrolled in my Journalism History and Theories class where a significant portion of reading material was dedicated to the critical analysis of the link between media, democracy, PR, and advertisement. In Henry's case, this created a real tension that would have been a challenge to deal with even for a native teacher.

When we read Walter Lippmann's (1922) passages on the increasing role played by the *publicity man* in the 1920s American journalism culture, Henry expressed a subtle level of anxiety. But two weeks later, when we discussed excerpts from *Manufacturing Consent* by Herman and Chomsky (1988), he became visibly upset to the point that he openly challenged my choice of the text in the classroom. His subsequent weekly reflection piece read like a satirical spoof, exaggerating the role of "evil advertisers" who day and night plot against the American public. "You obviously must think that the advertisement is responsible for all that is wrong with our society," Henry concluded in his essay.

I felt that this might become one of the defining moments in my teaching career. In the post-9/11 world, it is quite common to label someone as an anti-American element—and a nonnative teacher may indeed be an easy target. Yet, as a former journalist, I worked in three countries that have very different media cultures, and I am quite aware of the substantial impact that advertisement and PR have on the US culture. At the same time, Henry was one of our full-paying students and his Madison Avenue–generated tuition was contributing not only toward my salary but also financed my own critical research. And I was fully aware of the dialectic conundrum in which I myself was trapped.

But my ultimate concern was for Henry. As his academic adviser for three years, I knew him quite well and I did not want to alienate the young man at any cost. He visibly grew angry as the semester progressed, avoiding eye contact during our ensuing class discussions. My impression was that he was ready to dismiss me as some nut who was just angry at the entire corporate system. I increasingly felt that I was losing the frail bond of trust between the student and his teacher that Zinn (2000) talks about, which I would consider as my ultimate failure. In lieu of simple feedback on his essay, I wrote Henry a very personal letter, expressing empathy with his position and suggesting that he produce a final paper that would critically challenge the readings I was assigning during the semester. My only condition was that his essay would be based purely on reliable library sources. "OK, it's a deal!" declared Henry gleefully when he read my suggestion. "I will do that and I will prove you wrong!"

He never did deliver on his promise. Yet his final essay still turned out to be one of the best papers produced in my class. No, Henry did not espouse my point of view, but this time he treated the assigned sources with the respect that they deserved. A few days later he graduated and seeing him walking down the aisle, I recalled the words of my own grad school mentor: I had one single crack at getting this student to think outside the perimeter of the cozy world in which he was brought up, and I did my best to seize it. It is now up to Henry what he takes out of the vexing readings that he wrestled with so much in my class.

Conclusion

Just like the 1830s/1840s European travelers whose experience I mentioned in the opening passages of this chapter, I myself continue to face very similar challenges in the US classroom two hundred years later. A common denominator is the aversion to abstract forms of knowledge that, to a large degree, resonates with the system of US higher education and goes hand in hand with the present tendency of its gradual commodification. The students of US universities increasingly perceive themselves— and are also perceived by the administrators and some faculty—as "clients" who have a right to dictate the terms and conditions of their own college experience. The historical observations from the opening part of this chapter clearly indicate that such tendencies go beyond the subjective and time-limited experience of an individual. Indeed, they may be well described as endemic to the system and attributed to the underlying structural elements of the social environment within which US higher education operates.

Contrary to most of my colleagues whose autoethnographies are conveyed in this volume dedicated to the experience of nonnative English speakers in the US classroom, I am well aware that I do not have to struggle either with the issues of race and ethnicity, or face challenges of gender. The reader may thus use my own experience as a yardstick to assess what happens when those two or three additional structuring categories are added to the mix. Ultimately, my case reveals that the very fact of having a particular accent still inevitably calls into play stereotypes that are deeply ingrained in US popular culture.

Note

1. Among the most famous visitors whose observations I consulted are Alexis de Tocqueville and Charles Dickens, but also lesser known French political economist

Michel Chevalier, Scottish writer Thomas Hamilton, early English sociologist Harriet Martineau, and Hungarian Count Sándor Bölöni Farkas.

References

Ball, S. J. 2012. *Global Education, Inc.: New Policy Networks and the Neoliberal Imaginary*. New York, NY: Routledge.

Bok, D. 2004. *Universities in the Marketplace: The Commercialization of Higher Education*. Princeton, NJ: Princeton University Press.

Chevalier, M. 1839. *Society, Manners and Politics in the United States*. Boston, MA: Weeks, Jordan and Co.

Davies, B., and R. Harré. 1990. "Positioning: The Discursive Production of Selves." *Journal for the Theory of Social Behavior* 20 (1): 43–63.

de Tocqueville, A. 1898. *Democracy in America*, 4th ed., Vol. 1. Translated by Henry Reeve. New York, NY: Langley.

Ellis, C. S. 2004. *The Ethnographic I: A Methodological Novel about Autoethnography*. Walnut Creek, CA: Alta Mira Press.

Ellis, C. S., and A. Bochner. 2000. "Autoethnography, Personal Narrative, Reflexivity: Researcher as a Subject." In *Handbook of Qualitative Research*, edited by N. K. Denzin and Y. S. Lincoln, 2nd ed., 733–768. Thousand Oaks, CA: Sage.

Hamilton, T. 1834. *Man and Manners in America*. Edinburgh, Scotland: William Blackwood.

Harding, S., and M. B. Hintikka, eds. 1983. *Discovering Reality: Feminist Perspectives on Epistemology, Metaphysics, Methodology, and the Philosophy of Science*. Dordrecht, The Netherlands: Reidel.

Harré, R., and L. Van Langenhove. 1999. *Positioning Theory: Moral Contexts of Intentional Action*. Oxford, UK: Blackwell.

Herman, E. S., and N. Chomsky. 1988. *Manufacturing Consent: The Political Economy of the Mass Media*. New York, NY: Pantheon Books.

Lippmann, W. 1922. *Public Opinion*. New York, NY: Harcourt, Brace and Co.

Winter, G. 2003. "Jacuzzi U.? A Battle of Perks to Lure Students." *The New York Times*, October 5, A1.

Zinn, H. 2000. "How Free is Higher Education?" In *Campus, Inc.: Corporate Power in the Ivory Tower*, edited by G. D. White and E. C. Hauck, 173–179. Amherst, MA: Prometheus Books.

JURAJ KITTLER is an assistant professor of media, communication, and journalism at St. Lawrence University in Canton, New York.

3

This chapter discusses strategies to establish rapport and demonstrate knowledge in order to enhance instructor credibility and create a productive learning environment in the oral performance class.

Rapport and Knowledge: Enhancing Foreign Instructor Credibility in the Classroom

Mei Zhang

Introduction

As the world moves increasingly toward a globalized community, college students in the United States often take classes taught by international instructors who are either international professors or international teaching assistants (ITAs). Therefore, the college classroom has become an important site of intercultural communication. Researchers have produced ample literature on student communication apprehension and instructor credibility, power, and nonverbal immediacy among other general areas of inquiry (Richmond and Frymier 2010). Indeed, numerous studies have been conducted about measurement of source credibility (McCroskey and Young 1981). Several books have discussed teaching strategies and training models for international instructors (Bailey, Pialorsi, and Zukowski/Faust 1984; Nyquist et al. 1991; Pica, Barnes, and Finger 1990; Sarkisian 1997). However, few have examined international instructors' experiences and cultural differences from a communication perspective (Bresnahan and Cai 2000; Chen 2005; Li, Mazer, and Ju 2011). Thus, this chapter explores a neglected area of research: teaching oral communication. I argue that (a) establishing rapport and (b) demonstrating knowledge are the keys to enhancing foreign instructor credibility, increasing positive student perceptions, and creating a productive learning environment in the oral communication class.

In this chapter, I conduct an autoethnographic analysis of my own teaching based on twenty years of professional interaction with US students in the basic course classroom. Carr (2001), Crites (2001), and Gergen and Gergen (2001) emphasize the role of narrative in the articulation of human experience, retention of memory, and presentation of identity. Chase (2005)

NEW DIRECTIONS FOR TEACHING AND LEARNING, no. 138, Summer 2014 © 2014 Wiley Periodicals, Inc.
Published online in Wiley Online Library (wileyonlinelibrary.com) • DOI: 10.1002/tl.20094

states, "Narrative is retrospective meaning making—the shaping or ordering of past experience" (656). Likewise, Jones (2005) notes, "Autoethnography works to hold self and culture together" (764) and uses "personal narratives as auto/ethnographic texts" (785). Autoethnographic analysis can make sense only in the context of culture (Chang 2008). Coming from China and earning my PhD in the United States, I have taught public speaking as an ITA in a comprehensive university on the East Coast and oral communication as a faculty member in a regional state university in the Midwest. My journey as a female professor who has taught in both China and the United States provides a rich text for analysis and enables me to reflect on my teaching in the United States. Following Ellis and Bochner (2000), I focus on myself, the researcher, as the subject to interpret my experience in the larger intercultural context.

Various exigencies face both students and international instructors in the oral communication classroom. I believe that students growing up in the US culture tend to be individualistic, have low power distance, and engage in critical thinking to challenge authority and revise theories. Many might have a tremendous fear of public speaking. They are likely to be more apprehensive if their speech teacher is from a foreign country. Besides their speech anxiety, they worry about the possibility of ever being able to understand lectures and conversations because of the instructor's accent. Therefore, they may lack confidence in the instructor's ability to succeed in the classroom. Foreign accents certainly are among their utmost concerns. Indeed, people often consider international instructors hard to understand and attribute accents to a lack of intelligence and ability. Lev-Ari and Keysar (2010) have found that native speakers of English perceive nonnative speakers as "less credible" (1095). Floccia et al. (2009) conclude that it is difficult for listeners to adapt to foreign accents. Li et al. (2011) observe, "In essence, students' initial perceptions of ITA clarity, credibility, and language inadequacy coexist as constraining social structures that face ITAs in American instructional settings" (461).

Meanwhile, international instructors may also find a speech class particularly challenging and they are likely to experience communication apprehension and a sense of inadequacy. Hendrix (1997, 1998a, 1998b) conducted some of the first studies on race and teacher credibility and found that students used more stringent criteria to judge Black professors except when they taught ethnic studies courses. Black professors "perceived the extent to which they worked to build their credibility was greater than that of the White professors" (Hendrix 1998b, 44). Therefore, instructor ethnicity plays a significant role in student perception of instructor credibility (Patton 1999). Bazemore et al. (2010) state that international faculty's awareness of prejudice and discrimination against them contributes to their lower levels of self-esteem and well-being. Because of their foreign status, the ethos of their teaching position does not grant them due credibility as it does Caucasian American professors. Besides, many foreign professors look different and speak with accents, which may further set them apart from their American counterparts.

I was born and raised in China, where I internalized the values of collectivism, hierarchy, harmony, and utmost respect for teachers. When I began to teach public speaking in the United States, I had many concerns. Questions lingered on my mind. *How could I teach public speaking to American students, native speakers of English? Could they accept me? Would they be able to understand me?* Besides, nobody around seemed to know of Fudan, China's prestigious university where I graduated and eventually taught courses in English and international journalism before coming to the United States. Apparently, faculty and students wanted to know what I had done in the United States. I began to realize that I would have to start from the very beginning with my passport and my ITA status, having left behind my professional accomplishments in China. Even after earning my PhD from a US institution and finding a tenure-track position, I learned that my colleagues had an initial concern about my ability to be understood by students who had taken few, if any, courses with international instructors. Students were also asked informally about my speech clarity in the classroom.

Informed by Bitzer's (1968) definition of the rhetorical situation, this chapter considers the speech class as rhetorical because its various constraints call for my "fitting" response and provide an opportunity for me to make the class a transformative experience for students. I discuss two key strategies to enhance foreign instructor credibility and to improve teaching effectiveness: (a) establishing rapport and (b) demonstrating knowledge.

Establishing Rapport

Establishing rapport with students is the key to instructor credibility, contributing to students' positive perceptions of international instructors. Good rapport includes understanding, openness, role modeling, and appropriate use of space, each briefly explained below.

Understanding. International instructors' understanding of student concerns benefits teaching. Teven (2001) notes that teacher caring is an important part of teaching success. Understanding includes the dimensions of instructor availability, willingness to listen, initiative to help, and appreciation of student efforts. I make myself available in my office beyond office hours with or without appointment. I strongly encourage students to turn in their preliminary speech outlines and draft papers for comments before submitting final versions. Whenever a student relates concern about a grade, I take the time to listen and tell him or her to start remaining assignments early for my feedback. I make students realize that I am willing to help them even though grades depend on the quality of their work. Some instructors require students to wait at least 24 hours before making a grade appeal. I urge students to wait a day or two even though I do not require them to do so. If they insist on talking with me right away, then I listen to their concern in my office and make a follow-up appointment. I have certainly had emotional, irrational, and even threatening students. Nonetheless, I manage to stay calm, listen to what they have to say, tell them to reflect on my comments, and set up another meeting. In that way, the students do not perceive the instructor as arrogant or unavailable and the instructor appears willing to help the student.

In addition, I give encouraging oral responses to overall student work and individual speeches, if time permits. Written feedback is where I provide detailed comments. However, during my very first semester of teaching as an ITA, I did not quite realize the need to compliment students' efforts. I learned my lesson the hard way! I wrote all negative comments on students' first speeches and outlines. My criticism covered research, content, and delivery, hoping that such feedback would help them give better speeches the next time. I sensed that the students were upset with me. An informal class survey suggested that I was too negative. American teaching assistants suggested that I start with something positive before moving to constructive criticism. Since then, I learned to write positive feedback, such as compliments on student efforts or topic choices before commenting on weaknesses and giving suggestions for improvement. In that way, students feel that their work is acknowledged and appreciated even though it has room for improvement. I say "thanks" or "thank you" when they turn in their work. Though I did not use such words in China because students were expected to finish assignments, I heard American colleagues thanking students and indirectly learned the norms of teaching in the US classroom.

Openness.   International instructors need to exhibit openness and address students' curiosity about foreign cultures. Students have asked interesting, difficult, provocative, and even shocking questions. *Do you dream in Chinese? Do Chinese eat fish with bones? Do Chinese eat dogs? Why do you have a brother when the government allows each couple to have only one child? Do you have Chinese music as your cell phone ringtone?* I try to help them understand my experience and Chinese culture. After I became an assistant professor, I was initially frustrated when students would ask me if I had finished grading assignments submitted in the previous class period. When I said no, they would seem disappointed. One day, a student came to my office and said to me, "We know you are from China, but we know virtually nothing else about you. That's why we think all you do is teach and grade. We expect you to finish grading right away. You should tell us something about your life so we can know you better." Till then, I did not talk about myself because I felt that it would be a waste of class time.

Later, I deliberated and gradually realized that what the student said made sense. Because they knew nothing about my life, they assumed that all I did was work—only teaching with no research or family obligations. Their other professors probably shared personal information, which made me very different. I checked with a colleague and she told me that she let students know some aspects of her life. So I began to share family stories as a way to introduce myself and as a means to illustrate communication concepts. Of course, I keep openness at the appropriate level. When asked to comment on recent events involving both the United States and China, I usually give my thoughts on media coverage instead of offering my personal opinion. In that way, I am able to challenge students to think critically about media and at the same time I do not appear biased with my own personal viewpoint.

Role Modeling. International instructors should be role models for students because students are likely to be more critical of them than of American instructors. My rule is this: Lead by example if I expect students to follow my policies regarding punctuality, attendance, deadlines, and proofreading among others. I am punctual and usually go to class a few minutes early, which is one indication that I take my job seriously and I am organized and responsible. I also end class on time, knowing that students have only ten minutes between classes. I never miss a speech day. During severe weather, as long as the university is open, I am on campus, no matter what it takes me to get there. I am in my office, during office hours and beyond, grade student work in a timely way, and proofread my handouts and comments carefully. Students are likely to accept an accidental typo by my American colleagues while connecting mine to a poor command of English, consequently questioning my qualifications to teach as a nonnative speaker of English. Once a student complained that my grading was too tough. Though he did not challenge his grade, he showed me that my handout needed an extra space after a period. He might or might not have acted the same way toward my American colleagues, but I am inclined to believe that he perceived me differently. With my own role modeling, I expect students to be punctual, finish all assignments by deadlines, and show professionalism in their work.

Communication Space. Utilizing proper communication space is another important point in shaping perceived credibility of the international instructor. When I was growing up in China, student privacy was not a concern; in fact, teachers might comment not only positively but also negatively on a student's performance in public so as to encourage students to try harder. Eventually, I learned when to talk with students in the classroom and when to talk with them in my office. The classroom is the students' space where they perceive their own power; my office is my space that carries the instructor ethos. Students seem to make such a distinction. I answer general questions in the classroom setting; I meet with disruptive students in my office. If they want to discuss their projects, grades, or something personal, I see them in my office. In that way, I appear willing to take the extra time to help them while protecting their privacy.

As an ITA, I learned a big lesson about space and confidentiality. A student asked me in the presence of several others what I thought of her speech. She asked a question about her performance, so I answered it right away without thinking twice. I replied that her speech was quite good but then said something negative about her outline, unaware of the student's privacy concern. Her outline consisted of key words and phrases without complete sentences or proper reference citations. She said that she had learned how to write an outline in elementary school, did not need me to teach her how, and found my requirements "weird." A few days later, she told me that I should not have said anything negative about her outline in the presence of several other students after class. At that moment, I realized my inappropriate use of space and apologized to her. Since then, I have always answered students' questions about grades in my office. Proper use of communication space, together with understanding, openness, and role modeling, are essential to good rapport with students. Demonstrating knowledge is equally important to foreign instructor success in the American classroom.

Demonstrating Knowledge

Gass and Seiter (2011) state that expertise is one of the primary dimensions of credibility. International instructor knowledge in the oral communication class carries the professional and cultural dimensions and includes subject expertise, presentation clarity, and relevant knowledge.

Subject Expertise.   The key is to make students realize that international instructors are knowledgeable. Effective lecture organization and classroom activities aid knowledge presentation and student understanding of course materials. While I lectured most of the time as a faculty member in China, I now incorporate discussion, group work, Internet resources, PowerPoint slides, and question–answer time into my lectures. I also bring to class supplemental material and numerous examples not duplicated in the textbook. Whenever appropriate, I mention my own research in class. I am also very organized by following the schedule on my syllabus, never changing an exam day or a speech day. I usually give a preview of the lecture, summarize key points covered, and inform students about upcoming topics.

Furthermore, presentation of professional experience strengthens my perceived competence and credibility. I gradually overcame my uneasiness to mention my professional accomplishments after earning my PhD. I had assumed for a long time that students would know about my degree after reading the syllabus, but I was wrong. Several times, a student came to my office and saw my name preceded by "Dr." on my office door. He or she would say, "Oh, you are a doctor." I realized that I needed to tell them that on the first day of class. During the first week of class, I find time to relate my research and publications to students via my curriculum vitae on the university's website. Sometimes I show them journals and books I have contributed papers to.

Presentation Clarity.   While perceived subject expertise plays a significant role, perceived foreign instructor clarity is also of paramount importance. Foreign accents often erode students' perception of instructor expertise or intelligence. According to de Oliveira et al. (2009), students, especially those who have limited experience with international faculty, prefer American instructors to international instructors. Having a Chinese accent should not be my liability; helping students to put accents into perspective is the key. Positive perception diminishes negative connotation of accents. This example took place on one of my early days as an assistant professor. While I was discussing communication components, a student asked me whether my accent was an example of noise that interfered with the communication process. He implied that my accent made it difficult for students to understand my lecture. The question was surprising; all eyes were on me, with everyone eagerly waiting for my response. I said that it was a good critical thinking question and that my answer was yes. I told the class that I had made efforts to minimize my accent, I had learned to accept it, and that students normally did not find my accent to be a hindrance. The incident did not seem to affect my teaching evaluations negatively. In fact, my response might have contributed to positive student perception of me because of my openness and frankness.

Since then, I would mention that Americans tend to speak English with different regional accents and recommend the DVD *American Tongues* (Alvarez and Kolker 1988), which features diverse accents and dialects in the United States. My purpose is to show them that many Americans could be hard to understand. When time allows, we might discuss this topic in connection to nonverbal and verbal communication. I considered that student's noise question rude and inappropriate. Nonetheless, I answered it right away. I thought perhaps the student was indeed curious without being aware of his rudeness. I also wanted the students to know me better. That was about the only disrespectful question or comment concerning my accent which was directed toward me in the classroom. Students might have asked other inappropriate questions. I probably did not perceive them as such because of my willingness to help them understand Chinese culture better via my own personal experience. On the other hand, students would sometimes comment on my English and note that my English is better than that of their immigrant family members, other ITAs, or foreign professors. Such statements in class seem to have a positive impact on my credibility, judging by the students' numerical ratings of and comments on my teaching at the end of the semester.

Relevant Knowledge. Relevant knowledge is another important component of demonstrating knowledge. Students may not put the most emphasis on the instructor's academic rank, but they certainly prefer someone they can relate to and consider as credible. I made an effort to improve my linguistic abilities in graduate school by learning to understand American idioms, colloquiums, and slang, which did not appear in standard English textbooks in China. I accomplished this by watching a variety of TV shows and listening to Americans' conversations. I also paid attention to nonverbal codes in the United States, particularly kinesics and haptics because the Chinese of my generation acted differently regarding eye contact, hand gestures, and greeting styles. Another aspect of relevant knowledge is that of American culture: topics of interest to students such as mass media and sports as well as products that are important to local residents. I manage to keep up with such information by paying attention to various publications and online resources. Relevant knowledge also includes local information about campus culture, student life, activities on campus, and events in the community. I read campus newspapers, bulletin boards, and local newspapers. Finally, familiarity with new technologies adds another dimension to the relative knowledge of international instructors. I try to show that I am also a normal human being and am knowledgeable about matters outside my subject area.

Relevant knowledge enables me to connect with students and use examples to illustrate communication concepts. My credibility could be seriously damaged in a given semester if any of the following scenarios happens: not being aware of something that a student randomly mentions in class such as a movie, a product brand, or a celebrity's name; or accidentally referring to a city as a state. When such a scenario occurs, another student might explain what the first student mentioned or correct my slip of the tongue, which does not seem to change their perception of me. However, if nobody explains to me or corrects me, there is a possibility that the students might comment negatively on my knowledge of the United States on the teaching evaluation forms.

Reflections

As this chapter has shown, foreign instructors face unique challenges in the classroom; meanwhile, they have certainly added diversity to US higher education and enriched student experience. Nonnative English-speaking instructors with international backgrounds bring rich cultural diversity and new perspectives to the classroom. However, constraints such as accents and different life experiences can affect the instructors' perceived credibility and teaching effectiveness. Assuming that international instructors have the required English proficiency and subject expertise, this chapter has adopted a relational approach to teaching and identified two key strategies to increase foreign instructor credibility in the American classroom. The basic course taught by international instructors is primarily defined by the professional relationship between the instructor and the students. In other words, establishing rapport and demonstrating knowledge are paramount to positive student perceptions and success in the oral communication class.

This chapter indicates that international instructors need to constantly adapt to the ever-changing student body, classroom environment, and new media world. They should continuously find new ways to relate to students and present expertise, thereby impacting students' academic experiences and achieving improved understanding of American students. International

New Directions for Teaching and Learning • DOI: 10.1002/tl

instructors do not speak like native speakers of English or communicate exactly like their American counterparts, but with conscious efforts, even a simple smile or a "hello"/"how are you" greeting before class or in the hallway can show their interest in the students as individuals. An instructor with a passion for teaching and an upbeat attitude toward students is more likely to instill enthusiasm in students and make them look forward to the next class session, thus building and strengthening rapport with the students.

My teaching journey is a learning process with satisfactions and frustrations along the way. I have often adjusted my teaching style and the ways I present myself in the classroom in order to relate to students and meet the institutional criteria for teaching effectiveness. On the other hand, I have always upheld the principles of professional integrity and high academic standards. I may sometimes adopt strategies that my American colleagues use, but our seemingly similar approaches are rooted in differences—a non-native speaker's acculturated teaching style versus that of a native speaker. Those differences include dimensions, such as perceived credibility, verbal adaptation, nonverbal adjustment, cultural backgrounds, and life experiences in the United States as well as time and efforts needed for various responsibilities. Indeed, I constantly take extra steps to build rapport with students and reflect on my self-presentation in ways that other professors may not have to.

Future research may explore the following areas that this chapter has not addressed. One area of inquiry is the international students' perceptions of non-Caucasian international faculty credibility in the speech class. As US campuses become increasingly diverse, international instructors are most likely to teach international students in addition to American students in the classroom. After all, students from abroad come to the United States to learn English and, more than American students, they probably want to study with native speakers of English in an oral performance class. The other area is the role of humor in international instructor credibility in the classroom. I rarely intentionally use humor to make students laugh for fear of cultural misunderstanding. They do sometimes seem to find my statements humorous via their laughter and facial expressions; I just smile and get back to the topic under discussion. On my teaching evaluation forms, several students commented that I have a sense of humor while several others (fewer in number) suggested that I develop a sense of humor.

Conclusion

I have been teaching the oral performance course for twenty years—public speaking and oral communication. Because of space limitations, I have not been able to comment on course differences or the variations in the student body from one institution to the next. Nonetheless, I have identified common strategies that are generally applicable and important to international

New Directions for Teaching and Learning • DOI: 10.1002/tl

instructors in the communication classroom. In my academic career, stressful times enable me to grow whereas delightful moments bring me the joy of teaching. As one student noted, she learned from my class that foreigners are not "weird" but "different." Another student said that she wanted to visit China after taking my class. Whenever a student asks me about the meaning or spelling of a word, I consider that a time when he or she has forgotten about my status as a nonnative speaker of English and granted me the utmost credibility as a member of the American faculty. Such moments as well as commencements and honors convocations make teaching deeply rewarding and inspire me to make meaningful contributions to my students' learning experience. In effect, I want to believe that I have expanded their horizons by making them realize that foreign instructors like me can add to their education a dimension that native instructors cannot.

References

Alvarez, L., and A. Kolker. 1988. *American Tongues*. United States: PBS.

Bailey, K., F. Pialorsi, and J. Zukowski/Faust, eds. 1984. *Foreign Teaching Assistants in U.S. Universities*. Washington, DC: National Association for Foreign Student Affairs.

Bazemore, S. D., L. H. Janda, V. J. Derlega, and J. F. Paulson. 2010. "The Role of Rejection in Mediating the Effects of Stigma Consciousness among Foreign-Born University Professors." *Journal of Diversity in Higher Education* 3 (2): 85 96.

Bitzer, L. 1968. "The Rhetorical Situation." *Philosophy and Rhetoric* 1: 1–14.

Bresnahan, M. J., and D. H. Cai. 2000. "From the Other Side of the Desk: Conversations with International Students about Teaching in the U.S." *Qualitative Research Reports in Communication* 1 (4): 65–75.

Carr, D. 2001. "Narrative and the Real World: An Argument for Continuity." In *Memory, Identity, Community: The Idea of Narrative in the Human Sciences*, edited by L. P. Hinchman and S. K. Hinchman, 7–25. Albany, NY: State University of New York.

Chang, H. 2008. *Autoethnography as Method*. Walnut Creek, CA: Left Coast Press.

Chase, S. E. 2005. "Narrative Inquiry: Multiple Lenses, Approaches, Voices." In *The Sage Handbook of Qualitative Research*, edited by N. K. Denzin and Y. S. Lincoln, 3rd ed., 651–679. Thousand Oaks, CA: Sage.

Chen, G.-M. 2005. "Teaching Communication with a Foreign Accent." *Intercultural Communication Studies* 4 (2): 14–22.

Crites, S. 2001. "The Narrative Quality of Experience." In *Memory, Identity, Community: The Idea of Narrative in the Human Sciences*, edited by L. P. Hinchman and S. K. Hinchman, 26–50. Albany, NY: State University of New York.

de Oliveira, E. A., J. L. Braun, T. L. Carlson, and S. G. de Oliveira. 2009. "Students' Attitudes toward Foreign-Born and Domestic Instructors." *Journal of Diversity in Higher Education* 2 (2): 113–125.

Ellis, C. S., and A. P. Bochner. 2000. "Autoethnography, Personal Narrative, Reflexivity: Researcher as Subject." In *Handbook of Qualitative Research*, edited by N. K. Denzin and Y. S. Lincoln, 2nd ed., 733–768. Thousand Oaks, CA: Sage.

Floccia, C., J. Butler, J. Goslin, and L. Ellis. 2009. "Regional and Foreign Accent Processing in English: Can Listeners Adapt?" *Journal of Psycholinguistic Research* 38: 379–412.

Gass, R. H., and J. S. Seiter. 2011. *Persuasion, Social Influence and Compliance Gaining*, 4th ed. Boston, MA: Allyn & Bacon.

Gergen, K. J., and M. M. Gergen. 2001. "Narratives of the Self." In *Memory, Identity, Community: The Idea of Narrative in the Human Sciences*, edited by L. P. Hinchman and S. K. Hinchman, 161–184. Albany, NY: State University of New York.

Hendrix, K. G. 1997. "Student Perceptions of Verbal and Nonverbal Cues Leading to Images of Black and White Professor Credibility." *The Howard Journal of Communication* 8: 251–273.

Hendrix, K. G. 1998a. "Student Perceptions of the Influence of Race on Professor Credibility." *Journal of Black Studies* 28 (6): 738–763.

Hendrix, K. G. 1998b. "Black and White Male Professor Perceptions of the Influence of Race on Classroom Dynamics and Credibility." *Negro Educational Review* 49: 37–52.

Jones, S. H. 2005. "Autoethnography: Making the Personal Political." In *The Sage Handbook of Qualitative Research*, edited by N. K. Denzin and Y. S. Lincoln, 3rd ed., 763–791. Thousand Oaks, CA: Sage.

Lev-Ari, S., and B. Keysar. 2010. "Why Don't We Believe Non-Native Speakers? The Influence of Accent on Credibility." *Journal of Experimental Social Psychology* 46 (6): 1093–1096.

Li, L., J. P. Mazer, and R. Ju. 2011. "Resolving International Teaching Assistant Language Inadequacy through Dialogue: Challenges and Opportunities for Clarity and Credibility." *Communication Education* 60 (4): 461–478.

McCroskey, J. C., and T. J. Young. 1981. "Ethos and Credibility: The Construct and Its Measurement after Three Decades." *Central States Speech Journal* 32: 24–34.

Nyquist, J. D., R. D. Abbott, D. H. Wulff, and J. Sprague, eds. 1991. *Preparing the Professoriate of Tomorrow to Teach: Selected Readings in TA Training*. Dubuque, IA: Kendall/Hunt Publishing Company.

Patton, T. O. 1999. "Ethnicity and Gender: An Examination of Its Impact on Instructor Credibility in the University Classroom." *The Howard Journal of Communication* 10: 123–144.

Pica, T., G. A. Barnes, and G. A. Finger. 1990. *Teaching Matters: Skills and Strategies for International Teaching Assistants*. New York, NY: Newbury House Publishers.

Richmond, V. P., and A. Frymier. 2010. "Communication Education and Instructional Development." In *A Century of Transformation: Studies in Honor of the 100th Anniversary of the Eastern Communication Association*, edited by J. W. Chesbro, 310–328. New York, NY: Oxford University Press.

Sarkisian, E. 1997. *Teaching American Students: A Guide for International Faculty and Teaching Assistants in Colleges and Universities*, rev. ed. Cambridge, MA: Harvard Printing and Publications Services.

Teven, J. J. 2001. "The Relationship among Teacher Characteristics and Perceived Caring." *Communication Education* 50 (2): 159–169.

MEI ZHANG *is an assistant dean in the College of Liberal Arts and Sciences and an associate professor in the Department of Communication Studies at Missouri Western State University.*

NEW DIRECTIONS FOR TEACHING AND LEARNING • DOI: 10.1002/tl

4

This chapter argues that the most important thing for a nonnative English-speaking teacher is to have an open and positive attitude toward students. A teacher's willingness to work out problems with individual students, coupled with openness to students' ideas and criticism, should help improve students' negative attitudes toward the teacher, which, in turn, should result in better learning outcomes and teaching evaluations.

Open and Positive Attitudes toward Teaching

Chia-Fang (Sandy) Hsu

Introduction

Like other nonnative English-speaking teachers in America, I had to overcome many difficulties in order to become an effective teacher. The teaching evaluations from my students and colleagues reflect language-related problems and classroom management issues. I experienced disrespect from some students because of my accent and teaching style. I have survived all these hardships by having open and positive attitudes toward teaching. I have become aware of the weaknesses of my teaching and have tried hard to improve them. This chapter includes my reflective thoughts about my own teaching experiences, the research findings on the confirmation model of teaching, and the results from my interviews with students.

My Teaching Experiences

I have taught various courses such as research methods and nonverbal communication during the past decade in the United States. Students' disrespectful behaviors tend to occur in lecture-oriented rather than discussion-oriented classes. When the course content is difficult and students have to understand my lecture to earn a good grade, they tend to blame my accent or teaching style. On the contrary, when the class involves lots of student presentations or student-led discussions, my accent and teaching style become minor issues. Thus, in my lecture-oriented classes, I try to incorporate more group activities or student presentations, and provide more detailed lecture notes if possible.

NEW DIRECTIONS FOR TEACHING AND LEARNING, no. 138, Summer 2014 © 2014 Wiley Periodicals, Inc.
Published online in Wiley Online Library (wileyonlinelibrary.com) • DOI: 10.1002/tl.20095

Disrespectful behaviors also tended to occur when I covered the material at a fast pace. Students felt frustrated when I hurried up to finish my talk. Thus, I tried to avoid covering too much material in one class meeting. I also learned to always speak confidently as when I appeared unsure or tentative in my replies to students' questions, they felt confused and evaluated me as being a less credible teacher.

Besides language barriers, my nonverbal communication sometimes caused misunderstanding. Being a good listener is very important in Asian culture. To show my interest, I often nodded my head and used filling words, like "yeah" and "huh-huh," while listening to students' questions or comments. Students may think that I agree with them or I want them to hurry up to finish their talk. On classroom management, I avoid confronting students who seem to be hostile toward me. In my culture, if a student has problems, it is his or her responsibility to contact the instructor. But in the United States, it is normally assumed that it is the teacher who should take the initiative in asking students what they are upset about.

I feel very thankful for my university allowing me to grow from mistakes to become a better teacher and, even more importantly, a better communicator. As Kuhn (1996) pointed out, "Learning American-style good teaching can be a challenging process" (97). It involves a combination of skills, including information organization, poised stage presence, discussion leader/facilitator, and social skills. To improve my skills, I underwent the accent modification treatment,[1] observed my colleagues' teaching in class and learned their teaching style, improved my "stage presence" based on the feedback from my colleagues, acquired materials from teachers who have taught similar courses, and modified the course content based on students' comments. I think a good teacher is one who is willing to change and adapt his or her teaching style and course content to meet students' needs. Keeping open and positive attitudes toward other people's criticism will certainly help nonnative-speaking teachers overcome the obstacles and become better teachers.

I am very curious about whether the lessons I have learned from teaching American students concur with the current literature on teaching effectiveness and students' experiences with nonnative-speaking teachers. Thus, in the following sections, I review the research findings on the confirmation model of teaching and present results from student interviews.

Confirmation Model of Teaching

As I embarked on my research journey, I soon realized that my teaching experiences were consistent with past research findings about nonnative-speaking teachers. Besides improving language skills, nonnative-speaking teachers typically face the challenge of using less authoritarian, but more animated and interactive style when teaching American students (Kuhn 1996). One strategy, which is often recommended to nonnative-speaking teachers to increase students' receptiveness, is to establish positive rapport with students (McCalman 2007; Wang 1999/2000). "Caring" and "open-minded" attitudes were noted as the most important contributor to positive rapport with students (Wang 1999/2000).

These findings support the confirmation model of teaching for all teachers. Teacher confirmation involves communicating to students in a way that endorses, recognizes, and acknowledges students as valuable, significant individuals (Ellis 2000, 2004). Confirmation behaviors, which include responding to students' questions and comments, demonstrating interest in students, and using interactive teaching styles, have been found to result in less receiver apprehension, and greater cognitive learning and effective learning for college teachers (Ellis 2000, 2004). The more confirmation students receive from their instructor, the less fear they experience in class. With lower apprehension levels, they are more able to process information and learn the course material (Preiss, Wheeless, and Allen 1990). They are also more likely to have positive effect for their instructor and the course (Chesebro and McCroskey 2001). Teacher confirmation behaviors have also been found to result in less student challenge behaviors, higher motivation levels, and better teaching evaluations (Goodboy and Myers 2008; Schrodt, Turman, and Soliz 2006).

My own study (Hsu 2012) compared the influence of teacher vocal quality and teacher confirmation on student learning. My findings suggest that teacher vocal qualities were not the determinant factor in student learning. Instead, students' perceived lack of confirmation from the instructor and fear of not being able to understand the material were the major causes of unsatisfactory learning outcomes in nonnative-speaking instructors' classes. Contrary to Ellis's study (2004), which did not find significant, direct effect of teacher confirmation on student learning among native-speaking teachers, my study indicated a stronger relationship between teacher confirmation and student learning. This finding suggests that the use of confirmation behaviors is particularly important for nonnative-speaking instructors' teaching. Because of cultural and accent differences, students find it difficult to relate to a nonnative-speaking teacher, which, in turn, affects their understanding of course material. Nonnative teachers may have to try harder in building interpersonal relationships with students by more frequent uses of confirmatory behaviors, such as showing interest in students and taking time responding to students' questions. Confirming behaviors should help increase students' receptivity to nonnative-speaking instructors' teaching, which, in turn, should improve students' learning outcomes.

My findings also confirmed the perspective of teaching as an interpersonal relationship (Frymier and Houser 2000), and the importance of establishing positive rapport with students for nonnative-speaking teachers (McCalman 2007; Wang 1999/2000). As explained below, the findings from students' interviews revealed that developing positive relationships with students was more important for nonnative-speaking than native-born professors, and such high level of expectations on rapport may have come from the notion of getting something compensatory for the instructors' foreignness and accents (Wang 1999/2000). For example, several students had similar comments such as "because they speak differently, they must make it up by relating to us better" (Wang 1999/2000, 39).

Interviews with Students

In order to understand students' experiences of taking nonnative-speaking teachers' courses, I conducted semi-structured, in-depth, face-to-face interviews with twenty-two undergraduate students in different majors at a small-size university located in the western region of the United States. These students were referred to me by six nonnative-speaking instructors on campus. The instructors received the information about this study through e-mail, which was forwarded to their domestic American students.[2] Interested students then contacted me for an interview. Students were majoring in different disciplines: engineering-related fields (eight), education (five), physics (four), communication (three), and finance (two). The courses included both lower and upper divisions. The ages of interviewees ranged from twenty to twenty-six. Twelve were men and ten were women. The majority of them were seniors (66 percent), 23 percent were juniors, and 11 percent were sophomores. All of them were Caucasian Americans.

All the interviews were video-recorded because they were to be part of my film about improving communication with nonnative-speaking teachers. I produced the film with a professional independent filmmaker. Each interview lasted 15–20 minutes. I took notes while listening to the video clips of the interviews, highlighting key responses from participants that could develop into themes, and then transcribed key quotations verbatim. Thematic analysis was used to extract the most important information from the transcripts (Owen 1984). A list of themes was produced by clustering the common responses together.

My two research questions were: (a) what do students like most about taking classes from nonnative-speaking teachers? and (b) what difficulties have students experienced with nonnative-speaking teachers? For the first research question, most students commented that nonnative-speaking teachers were very willing to explain things over and over to help them out. For instance, one senior student in education commented:

> Usually they [nonnative-speaking teachers] are very willing to reelaborate something if you don't understand or are confused about what they are saying. They are pretty open to ideas. They are willing to give you extra assistance or even just to get to know you better more so than my native-speaking teachers.

Another senior student in education offered a similar view:

They [nonnative-speaking teachers] tend to repeat important information which gives you a chance to hear the due days and what is required in the assignment multiple times. There are multiple opportunities to ask questions and to confront the problems you have. They really reiterate everything and try to clear any confusion due to language difference or accent.

Besides willingness to help, students also appreciated nonnative-speaking teachers' enthusiasm and patience in the classroom and during the office hours. For example, one junior in physics described:

He is very animated, always active and smiling. He keeps asking if we understand. In that way, it keeps your attention. Every time I go to his office hour, he always shows everything step by step and tries to explain it very well. In the last leg I had to go in, I was completely lost. By the time I left, I understood it completely. He always takes his time. He doesn't rush through things like some teachers.

For the second research question, three students said that they did not experience any difficulty at all and everything was quite positive. For example, one senior student in engineering said, "some of my best professors are actually nonnative speakers and language differences do not affect my learning at all." Another engineering student had similar experiences and said, "Generally they speak English very well. One math professor struggled a little bit that time, but she turns out to be one of the best professors I ever have. Certainly there is a misconception that nonnative teachers are not able to communicate the information. Certainly they can."

Most students attributed the difficulties to the accent or language differences. For example, one sophomore in physics said, "At beginning I found a little bit difficult just trying to understand his accent. But after the first few days, I got used to it. He is very easy to understand." Another senior student in engineering also commented:

In some classes, how they pronounced certain words, especially in math class, got really difficult sometimes, because I didn't understand what they are saying. But after a while with them saying and writing on the board, it didn't become a problem anymore. I still have to go through the book and make sure the equations I wrote down are right. So it requires me to do a bit more work outside the class to make sure I heard everything correctly.

Besides trying to understand what the teacher said, a couple of students expressed their frustration of not being understood by their teacher. For example, one junior in finance said, "I have them in all of my math and physics classes. Sometimes when you ask a question, you have to articulate exactly what you are saying. Sometimes you have to ask twice to have them answered." Another senior student in education reported similar experiences:

> Sometimes because of language barriers, I feel the teacher doesn't quite understand what I am saying. One time I was simply confused with the reading. It doesn't mean I disagree or I thought it was wrong. But the teacher thought I did not enjoy it because it's different from what I normally thought. It was my first experience with a nonnative speaker. Now I learn that to practice my patience, I just need to take time to say actually this is what I mean.

Implications from Students' Interviews

Overall, these students appreciated nonnative-speaking teachers' helpfulness, enthusiasm, and patience, but acknowledged that misunderstandings occurred due to language barriers. These findings could help explain why students' disrespectful behaviors tended to occur when I rushed through the material to keep up with the syllabus schedule. When students feel that they are being rushed, it is not only harder for them to understand what I am saying, but also makes them think that I am so impatient when explaining the material or I care less about their understanding than keeping up the schedule.

The interview results were also consistent with my previous study (Hsu 2012), which demonstrated that although teachers' accent and other vocal qualities affected students' perceived learning, nonnative-speaking teachers could improve students' understanding by using more confirmation behaviors, such as showing interest in students and taking time responding to students' questions. When a teacher established good relationships with students, his or her accent or language barriers would become more acceptable by students, which, in turn, would result in better learning outcomes and teaching evaluations.

Recommendations for Nonnative-Speaking Teachers

Based on my teaching experiences, literature review, and student interviews, several recommendations can be made as to what nonnative-speaking instructors can do to make their teaching more effective. First, having open and positive attitudes toward teaching is most important for nonnative speakers to become effective teachers. I am able to become a better teacher because I take students' and others' comments into my heart, and am willing to change and adapt to what students need. The interviews also revealed that some students' favorite teachers are actually nonnative speakers because they are enthusiastic about teaching. To compensate for language barriers, students feel or expect that nonnative-speaking teachers show more enthusiasm and patience in teaching than their native-born teachers

(Wang 1999/2000). However, there is only so much we can do as a teacher. It is important to let students know that we have tried our best teaching the course and they need to respect us in return.

Second, several students mentioned that it took them a while to understand the instructor's accent. Nonnative-speaking teachers can slow down when giving a lecture, especially during the first few weeks of the semester. Besides slowing down, using clear visual aids are also helpful for reducing the language barriers. If students still cannot understand, I would provide more detailed written notes upon their request.

Third, we should create more opportunities for students to ask questions. For example, in both my undergraduate research methods and graduate statistics classes, I usually leave the last five minutes of each meeting for students to write down their thoughts over "how has your understanding been improved?" and "what do you not understand?" I then clarify the most common problems students have at the beginning of the next meeting. I also give short written answers to questions that are not clarified in class. Besides regular office hours, I try to make my time more flexible for students to make appointments.

Fourth, students appreciated that nonnative-speaking teachers repeated their explanations and used multiple examples during the lectures. I think it is very important to make the course content relevant to students by giving examples that they can relate to in real life. Especially in difficult courses like Research Methods or Communication Theory, students need to know how to apply the course content to solve problems in real life. Otherwise, they will not be motivated or interested in learning about the course subject at all.

Fifth, we need to be sensitive to our own and students' nonverbal behaviors/feedback. Deliver the course content in a style that will be perceived as a confident, poised speaker. Too many or too few head nods or body movements can be perceived as a sign of discomfort. Also, a good teacher is observant of students' nonverbal cues. Most students do not reveal their dislikes toward the class until filling out teaching evaluations at the end of the semester. If students' faces appear confused or they show no interest by looking away, the teacher may have to stop for a moment and ask them if anything needs clarification. If students seem to be frustrated or angry, the teacher should try to understand the problems and find out the solutions to reduce their frustration or hostility. Another useful strategy might be to solicit students' anonymous comments in the middle of the semester to gauge if everything is on the right track.

Finally, students felt that nonnative-speaking teachers helped them learn more about other cultures and become more globalized. Thus, talking about stories that happened in our home country or joking about our own accent not only increases students' cultural awareness, but also helps break down barriers. Likewise, we should appreciate the opportunities to learn more about American culture through teaching. In fact, students

New Directions for Teaching and Learning • DOI: 10.1002/tl

believe that nonnative-speaking teachers who openly solicit criticisms or show their willingness to learn aspects of English language or American culture are more likely to develop better relationships with their students (Wang 1999/2000).

Conclusion

Because of language and cultural differences, nonnative-speaking teachers face several challenges when teaching college students in the United States. To increase students' receptivity to our teaching, we should always keep open and positive attitudes, be willing to work out any problems with individual student throughout his or her learning process, and adapt our teaching styles to fit what students need. We should constantly praise students for good work, use a variety of techniques and exercises to help students understand the material, and show interest in responding to students' questions and comments. Being open and positive to students' ideas and criticism should help improve students' attitudes toward the teacher, which, in turn, should result in better learning outcomes and teaching evaluations.

Notes

1. I received the accent modification treatment at the Speech and Hearing Clinic at the University of Wyoming. I paid for the treatment out of personal funds. The treatment was given on a one-on-one basis, which involved identifying deviations in the person's current speech from the desired accent, changing the way one used the mouth, teeth, and tongue to form vowel and consonant sounds, and modifying one's intonation and stress patterns.

2. Students were informed of the general purpose of the study, interview questions, length, meeting time, and location of the interview; they were paid $10 for participating in this study.

References

Chesebro, J. D., and J. C. McCroskey. 2001. "The Relationship of Teacher Clarity and Immediacy with Student State Receiver Apprehension, Affect, and Cognitive Learning." *Communication Education* 50: 59–68.

Ellis, K. 2000. "Perceived Teacher Confirmation: The Development and Validation of an Instrument and Two Studies of the Relationship to Cognitive and Affective Learning." *Human Communication Research* 26: 264–291.

Ellis, K. 2004. "The Impact of Perceived Teacher Confirmation on Receiver Apprehension, Motivation, and Learning." *Communication Education* 53: 1–20.

Frymier, A. B., and M. L. Houser. 2000. "The Teacher–Student Relationship as an Interpersonal Relationship." *Communication Education* 49: 207–219.

Goodboy, A. K., and S. A. Myers. 2008. "The Effect of Teacher Confirmation on Student Communication and Learning Outcomes." *Communication Education* 57: 153–179. doi: 10.1080/03634520701787777

Hsu, C.-F. 2012. "The Influence of Vocal Qualities and Confirmation of Nonnative English-Speaking Teachers on Student Receiver Apprehension, Affective Learning, and Cognitive Learning." *Communication Education* 61: 4–16.

Kuhn, E. 1996. "Cross-Cultural Stumbling Blocks for International Teachers." *College Teaching* 44: 96–99.

McCalman, C. L. 2007. "Being an Interculturally Competent Instructor in the United States: Issues of Classroom Dynamics and Appropriateness, and Recommendations for International Instructors." In *Neither White Nor Male: Female Faculty of Color*, New Directions for Teaching and Learning, no. 110, edited by K. G. Hendrix, 65–74. San Francisco, CA: Jossey-Bass.

Owen, W. F. 1984. "Interpretive Themes in Relational Communication." *Quarterly Journal of Speech* 70: 274–287.

Preiss, R. W., L. R. Wheeless, and M. Allen. 1990. "The Cognitive Consequences of Receiver Apprehension: A Meta-Analytic Review." *Journal of Social Behavior and Personality* 5: 155–172.

Schrodt, P., P. D. Turman, and J. S. Soliz. 2006. "Perceived Understanding as a Mediator of Perceived Teacher Confirmation and Students' Ratings of Instruction." *Communication Education* 55: 370–388.

Wang, J. 1999/2000. "'Don't Lose Your Accent!': American Students and Their Foreign-Born Non-Native-Speaker College Instructors." *Intercultural Communication Studies* 9: 31–46.

CHIA-FANG (SANDY) HSU is an associate professor in the Department of Communication & Journalism, University of Wyoming.

This chapter presents an autoethnography of an international graduate teaching assistant (ITA) at two universities (in a midsize state university in the eastern United States and a large public research university in the southwestern United States). Standpoint and muted group theories are utilized to discuss the experiences of being a female ITA from Africa.

Opposite Worlds, Singular Mission: Teaching as an ITA

Consolata Nthemba Mutua

Introduction

The United States welcomes a large number of international students onto its university campuses every year. Many of them are graduate students, who along with their study contribute to the increasing ranks of *international graduate teaching assistants* (ITAs; Chalupa and Lair 2000). In many universities, *teaching assistants* (TAs)[1] assist faculty in the classroom and typically serve as "laboratory assistants, recitation or discussion section leaders, homework graders, help-room staff, and test proctors" (Plakans 1997, 95). Moreover, some advanced doctoral students who are readying themselves for academic positions are assigned undergraduate classes to teach where they are the instructor on record responsible for writing the syllabus, choosing textbooks, and creating examinations in order to gain some classroom teaching experience before they become faculty members.

The presence of ITAs in the US American classroom has given rise to complex issues in higher education, most of which are documented by *Teachers of English to Speakers of Other Languages* (TESOL) scholars and practitioners. There have typically been complaints from undergraduate students, their parents, and alumni (Plakans 1997), most of which have been reduced, in the minds of the larger public, to a linguistic one—that of English language proficiency and how this affects US undergraduate students' perception of the ITA and their subsequent success or performance in the course. Previous research has shown that such perceptions are often negative, with students reporting that their foreign instructors' accents are hard to understand and subsequently evaluating them as not as knowledgeable or skilled as US born TAs (Axelson and Madden 1994; Brown, Fishman,

NEW DIRECTIONS FOR TEACHING AND LEARNING, no. 138, Summer 2014 © 2014 Wiley Periodicals, Inc.
Published online in Wiley Online Library (wileyonlinelibrary.com) • DOI: 10.1002/tl.20096

and Jones 1989; Douglas and Selinker 1994; Shaw 1994; Yule 1994). ITAs from English-speaking countries are not spared either. According to Fitch and Morgan (2003), students also complained that their ITAs did not speak the "right kind of English" because they had accented speech as native English speakers born outside the United States (for example, India and the Caribbean).

This seemingly universal problem with ITAs has commonly been termed the "foreign TA problem" (Bailey 1984; Damron 2003). As Fitch and Morgan (2003) state, "the so-called 'problem' of ITAs is the stuff of legend with virtually every person who has attended a university employing ITAs having at least heard tales of incompetent ITAs who lack basic English-language skills and who exhibit a variety of poor classroom-management skills" (309). Other researchers have looked at ITA training programs (Hoekje and Williams 1992; Jia and Bergerson 2008) and general adjustment concerns experienced by international students (Al-Sharideh and Goe 1998; Furnham and Alibhai 1985; Sheehan and Pearson 1995; Zhai 2002). What is interesting is the persistence of this perception given that the results of research suggest "assumptions of widespread inadequacies in the language and teaching competencies of ITAs and dissatisfaction with preparation programs are unwarranted" (Chism 1987, 249).

Most studies focusing on international teaching assistants have been carried out by non-ITA researchers and focus on ITAs' performance and efficiency in the US American classroom, and look at universities' training programs for their ITAs, evaluations of ITAs' performance by the universities, and even undergraduate students' experiences in classes taught by ITAs. There is a gap in the literature for studies dealing with the personal experiences of ITAs, a fact that is thankfully being acknowledged, with studies authored by international academics focusing on their experiences in the United States coming out in the recent past. A previous volume of this journal, NDTL Issue 110, explored the experiences of female faculty of color and according to Hendrix (2007) sought to "[serve] as a reference for positioning women of color within the larger context of higher education" (1) explicitly moving female of color from "margin to center" (1).

Similarly, in this chapter, I explore my teaching of and engagement with undergraduates, a majority of whom are White/Anglo American, as an ITA at two universities (a medium-sized state university in the eastern United States and a larger research university in the southwestern United States). This chapter aims to articulate the real-life challenges, setbacks, and rewards that come along with teaching in an American classroom. I seek to "produce meaningful, accessible, and evocative research grounded in personal experience, ... that will sensitize [my] readers to issues of identity politics, to experiences shrouded in silence, and to forms of representation that deepen our capacity to empathize with people who are different from us" (Ellis, Adams, and Bochner 2011, 275) and "lay a foundation for more inclusive future research" (Hendrix 2007, 1).

NEW DIRECTIONS FOR TEACHING AND LEARNING • DOI: 10.1002/tl

Theoretical Foundations Guiding the Exploration of Life as an ITA in the US Classroom

As a female international student from an African country, I am part of the minority nondominant group in US academe. My identity has a profound effect on my teaching experience and is different from ITAs from other countries in various ways: my cultural upbringing, English language proficiency, and my educational and teaching experience in Kenya are distinctly different from those of an ITA from, say, China, Turkey, Canada, India, or any other African country. To better speak about my teaching life in the United States, I utilize standpoint theory (ST) and muted group theory (MGT). These two theories work well for this autoethnography because they center on marginalized voices, including those of women. In the next section, I touch briefly on each of these theories and explain how they guide my discussion of my experiences as a female, African ITA in the United States.

Standpoint Theory.   Emerging from feminist scholarship (Harding 1991; Hartsock 1983; Smith 1987; Wood 1992), this theory explores the everyday lives of individuals, postulating that we all occupy specific places in the social hierarchy—standpoints. Standpoints do not follow from our social location, but are "earned through critical reflection on power relations and through engaging in the struggle required to construct an oppositional stance" (Wood 2005, 61). These standpoints afford us a partial understanding of the social whole, with the exception that those who occupy the lower rungs of the social hierarchy have a fuller and more critical understanding of the social whole than those who are at the top. Similar in its focus on marginalized groups is muted group theory.

Muted Group Theory.   First proposed by Ardener (1975), this theory was further applied in discussing communication barriers faced by women (Kramarae 1981) and African-American men (Orbe 1998) and is encapsulated in the idea that groups that are on top of the social hierarchy determine to a great extent the dominant communication system of a society, leading to the "muting" of the marginalized groups. Subsequently, as Orbe (1998) discusses in his articulation of cocultural theory, cocultural group members find a way to engage with other groups within this dominant communication system, resulting in particular "communication strategies (for example, censoring self, utilizing liaisons, mirroring, confronting) that reflect larger co-cultural communication orientations (for example, assertive accommodation, nonassertive separation, aggressive assimilation)" (Orbe 2005, 66).

Standpoint and muted group theories provide a foundation for the analysis of my experiences as an ITA, as well as an understanding of the implications of biased or partial perceptions of ITAs and their contributions to the American classroom. These theories allow me to interrogate my marginalized positioning in American academia, providing me with the tools to analyze my own reactions as well as what is going on around particular events. Drawing on ST and MGT, I next discuss my experiences in the American classroom.

Linguistic Competence

The most visible aspect of the "ITA problem" involves English language proficiency. Most of the past literature has dealt with individuals for whom English was a second language (that is, a language that is not spoken in their home country and they have had to learn it especially to be able to come to study in the United States). My case was different as I am from Kenya. Kenya was a British colony and as is the case for most if not all former colonies, we adopted the language of the colonizer as our official language. Thus business, government, media, and education in Kenya are conducted primarily in English. Except in rural areas where for the first three years of school instruction is in the local language, all schools in Kenya use English as the language of instruction and include English grammar and literature as a subject at all levels. I learned two languages—English and Kiswahili— simultaneously because of the urban setting I grew up in. I regard English, of the British variety, as one of my first languages and so would most of my fellow countrywomen and men.

Thus, when I first came to the United States, I honestly did not expect to have anyone take issue with my English proficiency. I spoke very good English, if I may say so myself. Heck, I was the best English language/literature student in my high school graduating class! And I have a love of reading, which has over the years expanded my vocabulary. Imagine my surprise when I encountered individuals who off the bat, upon meeting me, decided I did not speak English well! And this extended from strangers to colleagues and acquaintances. My reaction was not one of understanding, but one of anger at what I perceived to be the ignorance and misplaced ethnocentrism on the part of those I was interacting with. It took me a while but I finally understand this in the context of MGT, which mostly focuses on power relations found in one particular site—language—claiming that not everyone has had the opportunity to participate equally in the generation of ideas that are encoded in any society's discourse (Ardener 2005). My foreignness automatically negated my grasp of the English language in the eyes of those I encountered.

Over the years I found that I had to adjust my speech when speaking to different people. This is explained by the communication accommodation theory that "explores the different ways in which we accommodate our communication, our motivations for doing so, and the consequences" (Giles and Ogay 2007, 325). Some people have had no difficulty adjusting to my accent, while others usually act as if they have to strain a great deal to understand me. As a foreigner, it is expected that I will speak "American" and if people cannot understand me, it is my fault. It does not matter that I am fluent in English; the group I belong to did not participate in the setting up of the discursive practices I now find myself in. Given that my perception of my English proficiency differs from that of many people I encounter in my capacity as ITA, how does that affect my credibility in the classroom?

New Directions for Teaching and Learning • DOI: 10.1002/tl

My Experience in the Classroom

Right off the bat, those who take my class can tell from my name that I am not American. They can deduce this right away because my surname does not sound White/Anglo. If they do not automatically jump to that conclusion, then the first time they see me, they may, and if not, once I speak, they definitely know, I am not American.

I have found something that mostly works for me with regard to any questions students may have as to my linguistic competence. I address this from the very first day of class. I introduce myself and where I am from. I then note that my accent is Kenyan and it may take a bit of time to get used to it if they have never heard it before. I then joke that my English is very British and get them to tell me some of the words that are different in American and British English. This usually introduces some levity to the discussion and gets most students engaged, and drives the point home that English has different dialects. I then let them know that if there is a time during class that I say something they do not catch/understand, they are at liberty to raise their hands and ask me to repeat/clarify. I emphasize that I welcome this and it would in no way upset me. This strategy has worked very well for me in the six years I have been teaching in the United States in two different states.

That does not mean that I have not had students, who in their evaluation sheets at the end of the semester, say that I was hard to understand. Thankfully, for my ego at least, it was always the one or two students each few semesters. And perhaps to them I was hard to understand, but what about the thirty or so other students in the class? How did they understand me? For me, the question is not whether my English is good/bad, because I know my English is impeccable, but rather, it is about what attitude my students take in regard to either adjusting their ears and/or their prejudices toward foreigners they automatically perceive as non-English speaking.

Being Foreign, and from Africa!

Closely related to issues of perception and how it affects understanding and receptiveness to differing accents is also the issue of students' attitude to people who they deem as *foreign*. Being labeled thus can have both positive and not-so-positive consequences. What do I mean by that? The positive could be that your students find the fact that you are from somewhere else fascinating and their curiosity leads them to want to learn more about that place and many other places they did not know about prior to interacting with you. The not-so-positive could be those students who are not open-minded, have a cast-in-stone perspective of where you are from, and woe unto you if it is not a good one.

Take me for example—I am Kenyan, but as is the case for a lot of people in the United States, Africa is subsumed into this single monolithic "place"

NEW DIRECTIONS FOR TEACHING AND LEARNING • DOI: 10.1002/tl

over there, associated with disease, war, famine, and "primitiveness." Unfortunately, many Americans think that those are the only things you can find on the continent of Africa, and I have been asked the most inane questions. My favorite is, "How did *you* ever learn English?" To which I simply reply, "I learnt it on the plane on my way here!" Sarcasm aside, I welcome questions about where I am from because even though I lament the general lack of information on my country and the African continent in the United States, I am not so full of myself that I expect everyone to know everything there is to know about Kenya or the African continent (I say that as some think Africa is a nation, not a continent).

Fortunately, over the years, I have become adept at distinguishing those who are genuinely curious from those who are not, and are speaking from a place of condescension and ethnocentricity. As explicated in standpoint theory, subordinate locations (mine as an ITA) enable group members to understand their social locations and those of more powerful group members (Wood 2005). Having this knowledge however is still testy for the ITA who encounters students who are oblivious of their ethnocentrism. How do you deal with someone who fundamentally does not respect you or your knowledge because you are from Africa, which is synonymous with nothing positive to them? I do not think that *this* is unique to only ITAs from Africa, but I think it is safe to say that Africa is a much-maligned and misrepresented place and is most associated with many of the ills that can afflict the human being, a result of the media images portrayed in the West. I have had evaluation feedback that sounded very condescending, as if the student tolerated me because I am not from here (that is, the United States), implying that I would turn out to be a better teacher and be more understandable with more time in the United States and once my "Africanness" was mixed with a dash of "Americanism," with one comment that was outright menacing, all in capital letters declaring that "THERE SHOULD BE NO FOREIGNERS TEACHING AT (BLANK) UNIVERSITY!"

I wish that particular student would have offered concrete reasons as to why having foreign instructors was so despicable to him/her. I can only speculate, or would rather want to believe, that this was a disgruntled student who did not do well in my class and sought to vent his/her frustration over my foreignness. Whatever the reason for such an unhelpful and frankly mean and rude comment, truthfully, being an ITA comes with self-doubts about whether students are evaluating your performance as a teacher or their perception of you and where you are from—the latter, which I argue, is mostly unique for ITAs and not US-born Anglo TAs.

Am I Such a Horrible Teacher or Are These Students Just Mean and Prejudiced?

My master's and PhD education has been in the United States. The phenomenon of TAs is a North American invention rarely found in higher

NEW DIRECTIONS FOR TEACHING AND LEARNING • DOI: 10.1002/tl

education systems in other parts of the world (Bailey 1984), and this means that most ITAs are not familiar with what this position entails. Further, being from Kenya, I was exposed to a pedagogical process much different from the US one. Back home, classes were big, with one professor whose word was the law. One did not question and you could only speak up if the professor acknowledged you. Given that Kenya is a collectivistic, high-power distance culture, the respect accorded to those of higher authority also meant a different style of engagement with teachers. The United States is an individualistic, low-power distance culture where discussion, questioning, and a more level and personal student–professor interaction style is encouraged. On the other hand, the Kenyan model of interaction involves sitting in class while the professor gives a lecture, and the only interaction you may have outside of class involves a few minutes of the professor's office hours (if you are lucky).

I encountered this difference in pedagogical processes first as a master's student at a midsize university in the eastern United States. It took me a while to speak up in class, and to this day, I am still negotiating the North American practice of calling professors by their first name—I still call most of my professors by their professional title. What does this have to do with my identity as an ITA? Well, the expectations of how I would interact with my students are definitely different as compared with how I interacted with my professors back home, and how I still interact with some of my professors in the United States. Initially, I thought it best to maintain the power differential in my class, by having my students refer to me as Ms. Mutua. I have gradually phased that out to a policy where I ask students to call me what they feel most comfortable with. So I get called Consolata, Ms. Mutua, Professor Mutua, and Ma'am.

So what was behind my change of policy regarding how my students address me? The US American system of education values feedback from students who get to evaluate their instructors at the end of an academic semester. A lot of emphasis is placed on these student evaluations, with decisions about classes assigned in departments, and academic job descriptions asking for copies of student evaluations come into play. Getting good student evaluations is important for continuing to be an ITA as proof of one's teaching abilities; however, there are various factors that need to be considered: you cannot determine how students will respond to you, and thus both ITAs and TAs generally will try to make their courses rigorous and student interactions inspiring and fair. We all want positive evaluations but how are ITAs to determine if students are evaluating them fairly as compared to native English-speaking TAs?

Early studies carried out on ITAs showed that those who used an authoritarian style caused resentment in students, and having excellent teaching skills (North American skills) was a necessity for positive student evaluations (Bailey 1984; Landa and Perry 1984; Shaw and Garate 1984), and it can be assumed that this is true even now. Thus, starting out as an ITA, one

NEW DIRECTIONS FOR TEACHING AND LEARNING • DOI: 10.1002/tl

already is disadvantaged, unless they are aware of these scholarly research studies and/or can automatically switch from years of a particular pedagogical process into the North American one. As I noted earlier, perceptions of students toward ITAs, stemming from language competency and foreignness, have been found to be mostly negative. Thus, how is an ITA to interpret student evaluations, especially as compared to their American counterparts, given that these evaluations have a bearing on the classes they will be assigned, and the academic positions they would be applying to? And is it fair to expect this of ITAs given the advantage TAs have by virtue of being from this country? Those are questions I have grappled with throughout my term as an ITA. I have oscillated between thinking the system is unfair to ITAs and to thinking "I am already here, I have to assimilate."

Now, I recognize that since I will never have any control over how my students perceive me, I will work on the things I have control over: making sure I am well-prepared and practicing a style of engagement with students that facilitates community, collaborative learning, and social change. Interestingly enough, my evaluation scores have steadily improved the longer I have been teaching. Is it a result of becoming more comfortable as a teacher/more familiar with the material, or have I assimilated into the North American pedagogical culture? I could say it is both, in my case. I have become more assured as an instructor, scholar, and researcher and this is evident in my academic work and teaching. I have also had to adjust to the US system of classroom management, which involves more discussions in class, less formal forms of address, as well as use of various pedagogical and technological tools.

Implications for My Fellow ITAs and US Academia

I cannot purport to have all the answers for exactly what makes the lived experience of an ITA so unique and what could be done about it to make ITAs' lives better within the US academic context. What I can offer is my own experience and insight on how I dealt with the challenges I encountered, and what has helped make my life as an ITA at the very least bearable, and at the most, successful. In line with the literature (Hoekje and Williams 1992; Jia and Bergerson 2008), I have benefited from ITA training offered by my current university (which was carried out in my first year as a PhD student and ITA and focused on cultural aspects), and I have learnt the best practices of classroom management. As a result, I have grown as a teacher, scholar, and researcher, which when put together, have shaped me into the ITA I am today.

On the other hand, I have come to accept that given my social location as an ITA in the United States, most of the change has had to come from me. I have had to undo years of cultural learning regarding who a student and teacher is, and how that relationship should be handled—whether it be authoritative or egalitarian. I have learned to strategically enact communication practices that fit into the discursive practices of US academia (Orbe 2005). I am speaking about my experiences because I believe that it is important for the voices of ITAs to be added to the discourse on US higher education. I hope it leads to collaborative efforts among all co-cultural groups to shape the knowledge base we all operate from with the realization that there is "no definitive form of communication for any co-cultural group" (Orbe 2005, 66) and what we have is an unequal hierarchy that should be dismantled.

Note

1. I distinctively use TA to refer to teaching assistants who are American, and ITA to refer to teaching assistant who are from other nations in the world and have a student visa permitting them to study in the United States. However, some of the literature I have cited subsumes both categories under the label of TA.

References

Al-Sharideh, K. A., and W. R. Goe. 1998. "Ethnic Communities within the University: An Examination of Factors Influencing the Personal Adjustment of International Students." *Research in Higher Education* 39: 699–725.

Ardener, S. 1975. *Perceiving Women.* New York, NY: Wiley.

Ardener, S. 2005. "Ardener's 'Muted Groups': The Genesis of An Idea and Its Praxis." *Women & Language* 28(2): 50–54.

Axelson, E. R., and C. G. Madden. 1994. "Discourse Strategies for ITAs Across Instructional Contexts." In *Discourse and Performance of International Teaching Assistants,* edited by C. G. L. Madden and C. Myers, 153–186. Alexandria, VA: TESOL.

Bailey, K. M. 1984. "The 'Foreign TA Program.'" In *Foreign Teaching Assistants in U.S. Universities,* edited by K. Bailey, F. Pialorsi, and J. Zukowski-Faust, 3–15. Washington, DC: National Association for Foreign Student Affairs.

Brown, K., P. Fishman, and N. Jones. 1989, November. "Language Proficiency Legislation and the ITA." Paper presented at the 41st Annual NAFSA Conference, Minneapolis, MN.

Chalupa, C., and A. Lair. 2000. *Meeting the Needs of International TAs in the Foreign Language Classroom: A Model for Extended Training* (ED 481 005). Washington, DC: U.S. Department of Education.

Chism, N., ed. 1987. *Institutional Responsibilities and Responses in the Employment and Education of Teaching Assistants: Readings from a National Conference.* Columbus, OH: Center of Teaching Excellence, Ohio State University.

Damron, J. 2003. "What's the Problem? A New Perspective on ITA Communication." *Journal of Graduate Teaching Assistant Development* 9 (2): 81–88.

Douglas, D., and L. Selinker. 1994. "Research Methodology in Context-Based Second-Language Research." In *Research Methodology in Second-Language Acquisition,* edited by E. Tarone, S. Gass, and A. Cohen, 119–132. Hillsdale, NJ: Erlbaum.

Ellis, C., T. E. Adams, and A. P. Bochner. 2011. "Autoethnography: An Overview." *Historical Social Research/Historische Sozialforschung* 36 (4): 273–290. http://www.jstor.org/stable/23032294.

Fitch, F., and S. E. Morgan. 2003. "'Not a Lick of English': Constructing the ITA Identity through Student Narratives." *Communication Education* 52(3–4): 279–310.

Furnham, A., and N. Alibhai. 1985. "The Friendship Networks of Foreign Students: A Replication and Extension of the Functional Model." *International Journal of Psychology* 20 (6): 709–722.

Giles, H., and T. Ogay. 2007. "Communication Accommodation Theory." In *Explaining Communication: Contemporary Theories and Exemplars*, edited by B. B. Whaley and W. Samster, 325–344. Mahwah, NJ: Lawrence Erlbaum.

Harding, S. 1991. *Whose Science? Whose Knowledge? Thinking from Women's Lives*. Ithaca, NY: Cornell University Press.

Hartsock, N. 1983. "The Feminist Standpoint: Developing the Ground for a Specifically Feminist Historical Materialism." In *Discovering Reality*, edited by S. Harding and M. B. Hintikka, 283–310. Boston, MA: Ridel.

Hendrix, K. 2007. "Editor's Notes." In *Neither White Nor Male: Female Faculty of Color*, New Directions For Teaching and Learning, no. 110, edited by K. Hendrix, 1–3. San Francisco, CA: Jossey-Bass. doi:10.1002/tl.268

Hoekje, B., and J. Williams. 1992. "Communicative Competence and the Dilemma of International Teaching Assistant Education." *TESOL Quarterly* 26 (2): 243–269.

Jia, C., and A. A. Bergerson. 2008. "Understanding the International Teaching Assistant Training Program: A Case Study at a Northwestern Research University." *International Education* 37 (2): 77–98.

Kramarae, C. 1981. *Women and Men Speaking*. Rowley, MA: Newbury House Publishers, Inc.

Landa, M., and Perry, W. 1984. "An Evaluation of a Teaching Course for Foreign Teaching Assistants." In *Foreign Teaching Assistants in U.S. Universities*, edited by K. Bailey, F. Pialorsi, and J. Zukowski-Faust, 89–100. Washington, DC: NAFSA.

Orbe, M. P. 1998. *Constructing Co-Cultural Theory: An Explication of Culture, Power, and Communication*. Thousand Oaks, CA: Sage.

Orbe, M. P. 2005. "Continuing the Legacy of Theorizing from the Margins: Conceptualizations of Co-Cultural Theory." *Women and Language* 28 (2): 65–66.

Plakans, B. S. 1997. "Undergraduates' Experiences with and Attitudes toward International Teaching Assistants." *TESOL Quarterly* 31 (1): 95–119.

Shaw, P. A. 1994. "Discourse Competence in a Framework for ITA Training." In *Discourse and Performance of International Teaching Assistants*, edited by C. G. Madden and C. L. Myers, 27–51. Alexandria, VA: TESOL.

Shaw, P. A., and E. M. Garate. 1984. "Linguistic Competence, Communicative Needs, and University Pedagogy: Toward a Framework for TA Training." In *Foreign Teaching Assistants in U.S. Universities*, edited by K. Bailey, F. Pialorsi, and J. Zukowski-Faust, 22–40. Washington, DC: NAFSA.

Sheehan, O. T. O., and F. Pearson. 1995. "Asian International and American Students' Psychosocial Development." *Journal of College Student Development* 36: 522–530.

Smith, D. E. 1987. *The Everyday World as Problematic*. Toronto, Ontario, Canada: University of Toronto Press.

Wood, J. T. 1992. "Telling Our Stories: Narratives as a Basis for Theorizing Sexual Harassment." *Journal of Applied Communication Research* 20 (4): 349–362.

Wood, J. T. 2005. "Feminist Standpoint Theory and Muted Group Theory: Commonalities and Divergences." *Women and Language* 28 (2): 61–64.

Yule, G. 1994. "ITAs, Interaction, and Communicative Effectiveness." In *Discourse and Performance of International Teaching Assistants*, edited by C. G. Madden and C. L. Myers, 189–200. Alexandria, VA: TESOL.

Zhai, L. 2002. *Studying International Students: Adjustment Issues and Social Support*. Accessed May 13, 2014. http://files.eric.ed.gov/fulltext/ED474481.pdf.

CONSOLATA NTHEMBA MUTUA *is a PhD candidate in the Department of Communication & Journalism at the University of New Mexico.*

6

This chapter presents findings from a qualitative study which investigated the perceptions of twenty-five ITAs toward US American undergraduates. The participant cohort comprised fourteen PhD and eleven master's students, of which, three were male and twenty-two were female ITAs teaching oral communication or a communication course requiring at least two graded assignments. The responses gathered via an online survey were content analyzed using Leximancer, a text analytic software program. We found that the master's students reflected more about issues pertaining to their own public speaking and confidence, while the PhD students were more concerned with the preparation and presentation of the course material. In addition to discussing these findings, one coauthor of this study adds her reflexive voice to the experience of being a nonnative English speaker teaching American students.

Capturing the Experiences of International Teaching Assistants in the US American Classroom

Aparna Hebbani, Katherine Grace Hendrix

Introduction

Prior to the past two decades, the implicit message within instructional literature conveyed that the teaching experiences of professors of color paralleled those of their White counterparts in the classroom. Such literature has gradually acknowledged the existence of more heterogeneity among professors (Allen, Orbe, and Olivas 1999; de la Luz Reyes and Halcon 1990; Hendrix 1997, 1998, 2007; Houston 1996; Jackson and Hendrix 2003; Ono 1997); however, the role of nonnative English-speaking instructors has yet to be fully explored even though international teaching faculty constitute an important part of the professionals at many US American universities being employed as either international graduate teaching assistants (ITAs) or on the tenure track. It is against this backdrop that this qualitative study was conducted investigating the perceptions of twenty-five ITAs toward US American undergraduates. The participants were about to engage

NEW DIRECTIONS FOR TEACHING AND LEARNING, no. 138, Summer 2014 © 2014 Wiley Periodicals, Inc.
Published online in Wiley Online Library (wileyonlinelibrary.com) • DOI: 10.1002/tl.20097

in teaching for the first time or were reflecting upon actual classroom experiences. We begin with a brief description of qualitative methods followed by an overview of our study design and findings. We end with the autoethnographic reflections of one of the coauthors.

Qualitative Research and Methods

Qualitative research moves across disciplines, fields, and subject matter and is committed to a naturalistic, interpretative approach to investigating some phenomena or phenomenon. Employing data collection strategies, such as interviews, observation, and questionnaires, the investigator attempts to make sense of phenomena based on the meanings people bring to them, hence, seeking an emic (for example, insider) view of a routine, event, process, or problem (Denzin and Lincoln 2007; Hymes 1977). Qualitative researchers follow a paradigm that acknowledges: (a) multiple realities, (b) the minimized distance between researcher and participant, (c) researcher as embodied instrument, (d) the presence of value judgments in all empirical work, and (e) specialized rhetorical framing of an investigator's findings (for example, word choice, such as understand and credibility versus validity and reliability; Creswell 1998). Richard and Morse (2012) observe that qualitative approaches to research are appropriate when "the purpose is to learn from the participants in a setting or a process the way *they* experience it, the meanings they put on it, and how they interpret what they experience, [and when] you need methods that allow you to discover and do justice to their perceptions and the complexity of their interpretations" (28).

So far, much of the ITA research was conducted within a particular university, but we were aiming to reach ITAs from anywhere in the United States with a broad research question: What is the experience of being an international TA assigned to teach US American students? Previous research has primarily gathered voices of US American undergraduate students or, more recently, examined teacher training options while ignoring the voices of the ITAs themselves. Hence, the aim of this study was to give voice to the ITAs themselves to gather their experiences in the US classroom teaching oral communication; given this, an exploratory qualitative approach was employed.

Study Design and Participants.   In early 2010, an e-mail was sent to members on a worldwide communication research listserv soliciting potential participants for this study. The e-mail requested readers to participate in an online survey examining the perceptions of ITAs toward US American undergraduates. The researchers sought study participants (eighteen years or older) who were ITAs in oral communication or a communication course requiring at least two graded oral assignments. Interested participants clicked on a link which took them to an online survey (see Appendix). A total of twenty-five ITAs volunteered to complete the survey. The participant cohort comprised fourteen PhD and eleven master's students of which three were male and twenty two were female. Table 6.1 presents participants' profiles.

Data Analysis.   To assess the topical content of the survey responses, a content analysis was performed using the Leximancer text analytic software program (Smith 2000; Smith & Humphreys 2006). Leximancer uses word occurrence and co-occurrence counts to extract major thematic and conceptual content from an input text. This automated process generates a tailored taxonomy from the input text which can be displayed graphically via an interactive concept map, or as tables indicating key concepts and conceptual relationships.

Leximancer is an alternative analysis methodology to hand-coding and is equally suited to the analysis of small or large datasets. Unlike alternative qualitative analysis tools (for example, NVivo) that require analysts to design the list of concepts and coding rules themselves, Leximancer generates its own lists and relationships.

Results

The Leximancer analysis made extensive use of the dialog tagging feature, which allowed categorical data, such as gender and student group (PhD or master's), to be projected into the Leximancer map to determine the correspondence of these groups to particular concepts. The findings below focus on an analysis on the participant responses based on student group membership—that is, PhD or master's.[1]

PhD and MA Group Differences.   As seen in Table 6.1, our participants comprised fourteen PhD and eleven master's students. The dialog tags "Student_phd student" and "Student_master's student" were used to build the second Leximancer plot. Five conceptually coherent themes were identified through this analysis, namely, public speaking/confidence, teaching, international experience, preparation and communication of course material, and students. Given the proximity of the dialog tags for the PhD and master's student groups, it can be inferred that the master's students reflected more about issues involving their public speaking and confidence, while the PhD students were more concerned with the preparation and presentation of the course material. The key themes that arose for both groups are presented in Figure 6.1.

Leximancer uses word occurrence and co-occurrence counts to extract major thematic and conceptual content from an input text. This automated process generates a tailored taxonomy from the input text which can also be displayed graphically as a table indicating key concepts and conceptual relationships. An advantage of generating the concept list automatically is that the list is highly reliable, being generated from the input text itself, whereas manual lists require checks for coding reliability and validity. Key

Table 6.1. Participant Profiles

Gender	Age Group	Currently Studying	Race	Country of Origin	First Language	Second Language	Region of the United States Where Currently Teaching
Female	22–25	MA	Hispanic	Germany	German	Spanish	East
Female	22–25	MA	Asian	China	Chinese	English	Midwest
Female	22–25	MA	Hispanic	Ecuador	Spanish	English	East
Female	22–25	MA	Asian	Chinese	Chinese	English	Midwest/North
Female	22–25	MA	Asian	China	Chinese	English	Southeast
Female	26–30	MA	Chinese	Malaysia	Mandarin	Malay	South
Female	>30	MA	Japanese	Japan	Japanese	English	South
Female	>30	MA	Caucasian	Germany	German	English	West
Female	<21	MA	Asian	Vietnamese	Vietnamese	Polish	Midwest
Female	>30	PhD	Black	Caribbean	English	English-based dialect	East
Female	>30	PhD	Asian	China	Chinese	English	Midwest
Female	22–25	PhD	Asian	China	Chinese	English	East
Female	22–25	PhD	Chinese	China	Chinese	English	Ohio
Female	26–30	PhD	White	Russia	Russian	English	East
Female	26–30	PhD	Asian	Korea	Korean	English	East
Female	26–30	PhD	Caucasian	Belarus	Russian	Belarusian	South
Female	26–30	PhD	Afro-Asian	Madagascar	Malagasy	French	North
Female	26–30	PhD	Asian	India	Tamil	English	Southwest
Female	>30	PhD	Japanese	Japan	Japanese	English	South
Female	>30	PhD	Asian	India	Hindi	English	Southeast
Female	>30	PhD	Caucasian	Austria	German	English	East
Female	>30	PhD	Caucasian	Germany	German	English	Midwest
Male	22–25	MA	White	Netherlands	Dutch	Hebrew	Northeast
Male	26–30	MA	Arab	Morocco	Arabic	French	Midwest
Male	26–30	PhD	Caucasian	Denmark	Danish	English	Upper Midwest

Figure 6.1. Leximancer Plot Indicating the Relative Positioning of PhD and Master's Students to Major Themes Extracted from the Survey Responses

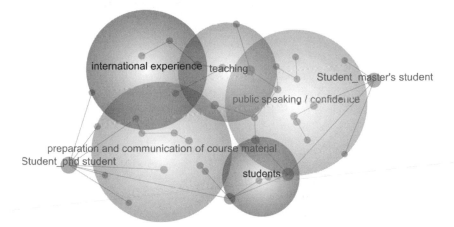

Table 6.2. Top 5 Concept Pairings by Current Level of Study

Master's ITAs (11)	PhD ITAs (14)
Public and speaking	Different and student
Feel and nervous	Teach and communication
Different and classroom	Material and knew
Public and instructor	Time and better
American and nervous	Material and accent

responses that highlight these concerns and the top five concept pairings for each group are reproduced in Table 6.2.

Master's Students.   As seen in Table 6.2, the master's students reflected more about issues of public speaking and confidence. Most were aware that their English language proficiency and cultural difference would come under scrutiny, but they also saw this as an opportunity to educate their US American students about other cultures. As a Chinese female ITA (22–25 years) stated, she was most afraid of "speaking a foreign language in public, especially [if] the listeners are native [English] speakers." The Malaysian Chinese MA student (26–30 years) who had been teaching for five semesters also felt that, "It's not easy for [an] ITA to teach American students as students usually complain about their ITA's English efficiency."

For some, their perceived lack of confidence was a hurdle they had to overcome perhaps due to limited teaching experience—as a Japanese female said "I try to appear confident (even though I don't have much confidence). I look at students' faces and talk loud enough." A German female (22–25 years) narrated similar sentiments, "After the second class meeting, my confidence level suddenly went down. I felt overwhelmed and believed that I was not capable to teach this class."

On the question "Which aspect of you do students react most adversely to: gender, size, race, nationality, age, or something else?" a German female (22–25 years) responded:

> I believe nationality. I had a response from a student last semester that read: Course assignments did not come across enough. I believe that is because my TA is not an English native. I think that a public speaking class should at least have a good public speaker . . . [I am not quoting directly] That made me very sad and angry.

One of the Japanese female participants (over thirty years) was cognizant of the cultural distance between her country of origin and the United States. She was mindful of the role that culture played in her oral communication classroom when she said, "Culturally, we need to appreciate American culture: individualism, discussion-based teaching, low-context, and low-power distance."

PhD Students. In comparison to their master's counterparts, the PhD students were more concerned with the preparation and presentation of the course material. This quote by a Danish male (26–30 years) encapsulates such focus, "I naturally made sure I knew the material in and out and did my best to incorporate a variety of different activities that were typical of the class early on in order to give everyone fair grounds for assessment." He prepared for teaching by reflecting on his own in-class experiences, "Thinking back to my own first days of class as an undergrad (and in graduate seminars), I thought about what the key elements of a good first impression of a class was and tried to convey a taste of the material, the requirements, the objectives, and the climate of ideas in which they would be operating. Most importantly, perhaps, I thought of ways to set the tone for the class in terms of atmosphere and classroom interaction."

Another strategy applied to improve confidence was to invest in material preparation as the Malagasy female (26–30 years) explained, "Getting prepared before class: Practicing my PowerPoint out loud—articulating words intelligibly. I usually asked my significant other to help me with unfamiliar words so that I knew how to pronounce them." The Chinese female ITA (22–25 years) used another strategy to win over her students. She ensured that she came across as absolutely confident (even though she was quite young). In addition, she told her students personal stories and experiences about being in America, which really interested her students. Overall, it appeared that the PhD students were [more] confident of themselves than their master's counterparts. As one Chinese female (over thirty years) pointed out, "Teaching experience does matter. It adds up to my credibility and confidence."

New Directions for Teaching and Learning • DOI: 10.1002/tl

Years of Teaching.   Next, we wanted to investigate whether we would find any difference based upon years of teaching. The responses to the question "How many semesters have you taught this course?" were used to segment the data and determine if particular concepts have a higher affinity to the number of semesters that ITAs taught. For instance, would such analyses show that novice ITAs would be more nervous and less confident as compared to the experienced ITAs who had three years of teaching experience? The results were somewhat inconclusive and did not show any significant patterns of difference with the high number of responses from ITAs in semester 2, and low number in semester 3 accounting for the significant variance in the results. One could conclude from this result that insufficient data means that a clear result is unobtainable with this set of participants.

Discussion, Autoethnographic Reflections, and Implications

The aim of this study was to gather the voices of ITAs in the US American classroom who taught oral communication courses. Thus, while the primary aim was not to look at categorical data, we found that the experiences of male and female ITAs who were in their master's and PhD program differed and offered us unique insights into how they viewed themselves in the oral communication classroom. This particular report focuses on the distinctions found based on graduate status—MA versus PhD. Table 6.2 shows us how both cohorts varied in their approach and focus as ITAs in the classroom. Clearly, the concept pairings (Table 6.2) indicate that doctoral students (most of whom were over thirty years) were more focused on their classroom delivery than the MA students (most of who were in the 22–25 years age group). The younger cohort appeared to be lacking confidence and doubting how their own communication would be perceived by their US American students.

Autoethnographic Reflections.   Reflecting upon my own experiences in the US classroom, an Indian woman entering a classroom at a Southern university was not easy. For a start, I was not male, I was not White, and I spoke with an Indian accent. Even though I was educated with English as my first language, during initial interactions, most students would assume that I was not fluent in English. In fact, come to think of it, I was, and am still, most efficient in English even though I speak three Indian languages and can understand two more.

I completed my master's degree in communication when I was twenty-seven years old, and started working as an ITA. A year later, I started my PhD studies at the same institution. Thus, by the time I started my PhD, I was twenty-nine years old and had grown leaps and bounds in terms of my maturity in an academic environment. Having been an ITA at the MA and PhD level, I can relate to experiences of our MA and PhD participants. Reflecting back to the first oral communication class I taught, I had just graduated from my master's program, had just delivered a baby, and was waiting to start my doctoral studies. Not having taught oral communication before was a huge challenge, but at the same time, it was exciting! I spent many days before that first class being nervous, reading the required chapters over and over, preparing overhead slides (this was before we had PowerPoint in the classroom), and wondering what I would wear. Making that jump from being seated in front of the instructor to being the instructor was nerve-wracking but something I knew I had to navigate through if I was to continue my life in academia.

I was able to overcome my anxiety and prepare myself for stepping into the oral communication classroom thanks to the rigorous ITA training that was offered in our department. Knowing what to expect and how to handle issues in the classroom with other ITAs who were in the same position as me helped me realize that I was not alone and that I could do it! But in hindsight, what was more challenging was to be able to "communicate" my competency to a classroom with mostly African-American undergraduate students. Not only did I think that my students found some difficulty in understanding my accent but also I confess that I struggled with understanding their accents.[2] This was a real issue I had to overcome if I was to grade their speeches! Listening closely to speeches and taping them so I could replay them was one strategy I applied to close this gap. I had to do my job well as it was an issue of me demonstrating credibility to teach an English oral communication course as an ITA. By this point in time, having been in the United States for three years, I was slowly able to relate to examples students used in their speeches. I also learnt quickly that showing some knowledge of American football helped build rapport with my male students; my female students were always eager to learn more about my being a new mother.

From my standpoint, I had to build an intercultural relationship in the classroom to lessen any perceptions of difference that students might have. I had to ensure that my grading was all done on time, I was punctual to class, I was well prepared, I was fair, and I had time before and after class to meet with students. Perhaps all TAs are mindful of doing the same, but as a female ITA, I felt that I was under extra scrutiny to prove myself, otherwise, I could easily have been a prime example of why ITAs should not teach communication courses.

Over time, once the trust and confidence was built both ways, my focus then moved from the micro issues (such as accent, being on time, being fair in grading, etc.) to macro issues, such as course content. By now I had started my PhD, and I devoted more time to prepping on how to make the course more "user-friendly" to students, especially those who were fearful of public speaking. As a woman, the first task at hand when coming across such a student was to put him/her at ease and build rapport with them. In some cases, I actually had the student make one presentation after class with only me in the room. When the students themselves realized that they had done better than they expected, the confidence grew and from then on, they were able to make the rest of the presentations in front of the whole class. I also learnt to keep meticulous records in case disgruntled students came back with a grade appeal at the end of the semester. Such strategies, coupled with experience, increased my confidence; on the other hand, over time, word got around among students on who was a good instructor, and in most classes, having to establish my credibility became less of an issue.

Implications.   Coming back to this study, we are cognizant that a significant majority of participants in our study were female and future studies with more male ITA participants may have different findings. Despite this limitation, the value of this *exploratory* work lies in its investigating an often overlooked aspect of teaching—the perceptions of the ITA themselves. One of the strengths of this study is that delivering the survey via an online platform made it possible to solicit ITAs from all over the country, and not just one university or state. So in that sense, this study provides a macro view of the ITA experience regardless of their geographical location. Secondly, having twenty-five participants is enough to garner a sense of ITAs' perspectives about being in the oral communication classroom. We also see a fairly equal spread of MA and PhD ITAs who come from various regions of the world.

Does visible difference then impact how the non-Anglo looking ITA perceives him/herself and compares their experience with the Anglo-background ITAs? Thus, it would be interesting for future researchers to explore, compare, and contrast the classroom experience between ITAs and US American TAs. Critics may say *everyone* is nervous so this is no big discovery. Our response to such a stance would be that this is exploratory and we can note nervousness is typical, but the extent, the length of time it lasts, coping mechanisms, and means of improving *might* differ between US American TAs and ITAs. Additionally, future researchers might want to compare/contrast whether classroom experiences of ITAs are impacted by skin color. This study has also made a valuable contribution to the field of ITA research by using a qualitative approach to study these participants; however, it would be equally valuable to study the ITA experience by possibly introducing quant and/or mixed methods to study this group and topic.

Conclusion

In closing, the aim of this qualitative study was to investigate the perceptions of ITAs toward US American undergraduates who were about to engage in teaching for the first time or were reflecting upon actual classroom experiences. Capturing the voice of this vastly muted group from various US states and institutions fills a gap in existent instructional literature. Findings from this exploratory study found that ITAs who were enrolled in a master's program were more cognizant of their self as compared to ITAs who were enrolled in a PhD program; the ITAs doing their PhD were also more focused on course materials and subject content than self.

Notes

1. Content analysis also mapped gender-based difference among the participants; however, those results are not discussed within this chapter.
2. They likely perceived a heavy Indian accent in me whereas I had difficulty quickly understanding what I interpreted as a thick, Southern Delta accent. Over time, I realize there were actually several accents depending on where students grew up in the tristate region or even by neighborhood within the city.

References

Allen, B. J., M. P. Orbe, and M. R. Olivas. 1999. "The Complexity of Our Tears: Dis/Enchantment and (in)Difference in The Academy." *Communication Theory* 9: 401–429.

Creswell, J. W. 1998. *Qualitative Inquiry and Research Design: Choosing Among Five Traditions.* Thousand Oaks, CA: Sage.

de la Luz Reyes, M., and J. J. Halcon. 1990. "Racism in Academia: The Old Wolf Revisited." In *Racism in Education*, edited by N. M. Hidalgo, C. L. McDowell, and E. V. Siddle, 69–83. Cambridge, MA: Harvard Educational Review.

Denzin, N. K., and Y. S. Lincoln. 2007. *Landscape of Qualitative Research*, 3rd ed. Thousand Oaks, CA: Sage.

Hendrix, K. G. 1997. "Student Perceptions of Verbal and Nonverbal Communication Cues Leading to Images of Professor Credibility." *Howard Journal of Communication* 8: 251–274.

Hendrix, K. G. 1998. "Student Perceptions of the Influence of Race on Professor Credibility." *Journal of Black Studies* 28: 738–763.

Hendrix, K. G., ed. 2007. *Neither White Nor Male: The Inter/Cross-Cultural Experiences of Female Faculty of Color in Academia.* New Directions in Teaching and Learning, no. 110. San Francisco, CA: Jossey-Bass.

Houston, M. 1996. "Beyond Survival on Campus: Envisioning Communication Studies at Women-Centered Universities." *Communication Education* 45: 338–342.

Hymes, D. H. 1977. "Qualitative/Quantitative Research Methodologies in Education: A Linguistic Perspective." *Anthropology & Education Quarterly* 8 (3): 165–176.

Jackson, R. L., II, and K. G. Hendrix. 2003. "Racial, Cultural, and Gendered Identities in Educational Contexts: Communication Perspectives on Identity Negotiation" [Special Issue]. *Communication Education* 52: 177–317.

Ono, K. A. 1997. "A Letter/Essay I've Been Longing to Write in My Personal/Academic Voice." *Western Journal of Communication* 61: 114–125.

Richard, M. G., and J. M. Morse. 2012. *Readme First for a User's Guide to Qualitative Methods.* Los Angeles, CA: Sage.

Smith, A. E. 2000, December. "Machine Mapping of Document Collections: The Leximancer System." Paper presented at the Proceedings of the Fifth Australasian Document Computing Symposium, Sunshine Coast, Australia.

Smith, A. E., and M. S. Humphreys. 2006. "Evaluation of Unsupervised Semantic Mapping of Natural Language with Leximancer Concept Mapping." *Behavior Research Methods* 38 (2): 262–279. doi: 10.3758/BF03192778

Aparna Hebbani is a lecturer in School of Journalism & Communication, The University of Queensland.

Katherine Grace Hendrix is a professor at University of Memphis.

Appendix

Demographics:
Male ___ Female___
Age range: 21 and under ___ 22–25 ___ 26–30 ___ Over 30 years ___
Master's student ___ PhD student ___
Race _____
Country of origin _____
1st Language _____
2nd Language _____
Region of United States (North, South, East, and West) that you currently reside in _____

PLEASE COMPLETE THIS PART OF THE SURVEY AS YOU REFLECT UPON THE FIRST FEW WEEKS OF SEMESTER AND RECENT CLASS PERIODS

EXPERIENCES BEFORE CLASS

1. Are you responding to your experience teaching an oral communication (public speaking) class? Y N
2. Are you responding to your experience teaching some other communication course that requires graded oral presentations? Y N
3. How many semesters have you taught the aforementioned course?
4. Have you taught any other communication courses? If yes, please specify the course name._____ _____ _
5. What was most helpful to you as you began to teach for the first time?
6. How did you prepare for the first day of class?
7. When you were preparing for the first day of class, did you think about the rest of the week? Explain.
8. What, if anything, were you thinking about your students?
9. Before the first day of teaching, what did you expect your US students would be like?
10. How were you feeling emotionally as you prepared to start the first day of class?
11. What was your biggest fear during the first few weeks?
12. What was your biggest accomplishment during the first few weeks?
13. When you walk into the classroom, how do you let American students see you? How do you present yourself?
14. Which aspect of you do students react most adversely to: gender/size/race/nationality/age/something else?
15. Similarly, are there aspects of your students that you react to?
16. Do you consult with each other (fellow ITAs) for assistance?
17. Do you ask for help from the course director?

EXPERIENCES AFTER THE INITIAL WEEKS OF CLASS:

1. How <u>did</u> you feel after a class is over?
2. Were you happy with your teaching? Please explain.
3. What were you thinking as you were teaching?
4. What were your thoughts about your students?
5. After teaching each lesson, how did you prepare for the next lecture?
6. Any other thoughts?

OVERVIEW

1. What are your thoughts about being an international TA assigned to teach US American students?
2. Has teaching become easier over time? Please explain.
3. What advice would you offer to a new ITA being assigned to teach an oral communication course for the first time?
4. If you were an ITA from a different nationality, for example, would your classroom experiences be similar? Please explain.

7

Globalization and recent demographic changes in the United States contribute to an increasing number of nonnative speakers of English in our classrooms. Such multicultural classrooms present different dynamics and challenges. Most teachers don't receive training in college to work with students whose first language and culture are different from their own. Perceiving the need to be better prepared to meet the learning needs of their incoming student population, these teachers chose to pursue the English as a Second Language certification. This chapter explores teachers' perceptions and experiences while learning content of a prerequisite intercultural course. The author, an international instructor, closes the chapter with her own reflections about the context.

International Instructor Preparing Teachers for Multicultural Classrooms in the United States: Teaching Intercultural Communication Competence Online

Claudia L. McCalman

Introduction

Globalization in education directly affects students and instructors in their teaching and learning experiences. Global awareness, interest for world affairs, and studying a second language are crucial to equip students with proper skills needed in the global workforce. As McGray (2006) explains, "We can't continue to be surrounded by foreign languages, cultures, and goods while young Americans remain hopelessly uninformed about the world beyond their borders" (42). He believes that the culprits for this situation have been the school system, curriculum, and low emphasis on foreign languages and world topics. A global awareness orientation in the curriculum involves new strategies, policies, and plans that prepare young people and teachers to be engaged in the multicultural classroom (see Bernardo and Malakolunthu 2013; McCall and Vang 2012). Most Caucasian students in the United States tend to have minimal interaction with people of other American cocultures or internationals before college (Orfield and

New Directions for Teaching and Learning, no. 138, Summer 2014 © 2014 Wiley Periodicals, Inc.
Published online in Wiley Online Library (wileyonlinelibrary.com) • DOI: 10.1002/tl.20098

Kurlaender 2001); this can negatively affect the preparation of our future global workforce. This lack of intercultural interaction begins early and can become a disadvantage in the development of traits such as receptivity, curiosity, motivation, and tolerance (see Bowman 2010). Fortunately, in the last few years, curriculum standards for both schools and universities are increasingly adding more emphasis on global awareness (Gopal 2011).

The purpose of this chapter is to highlight the importance of equipping American K–12 teachers with skills to face typical challenges of multicultural classrooms. Further, it reports teachers' insights and experiences while taking an intercultural communication course for their English as a Second Language (ESL) certification at a state university.

In sum, this chapter is organized into two basic sections. The first addresses the significance of the topic and multicultural classrooms challenges. The second reports a pilot study I conducted while teaching the intercultural course to these teachers. Finally, the chapter closes with my reflections in the role of international instructor and researcher.

The Multicultural Learning Environment

While our domestic students need to think beyond US borders, students who used to live beyond US borders are increasingly entering US classrooms. Changes in the US demographics alter classroom composition turning them into multicultural places (Education Week 2009). Nevertheless, in the next decade our projections indicate that our teacher population will remain mainly Caucasian (Villegas and Lucas 2007). Linguistic and cultural differences between students and teachers, if ignored, can deter the learning process.

Is it really necessary to be aware of cultural and language issues for effective teaching? Teachers make instructional decisions impacting on how students perceive their cultures, the culture of others, their nation, and the lives of people and events around the world (Merryfield and Kasay 2004). Teachers need to be equipped to teach ESL students because their instructional decisions will influence classroom climate, student achievement, and school success. Furthermore, "teacher beliefs about students significantly shape the expectations they hold for students' learning" (Villegas and Lucas 2007, 31) and consequently impact students' progress (Johnson 1995). Thus, teachers' intercultural preparation and professional development are important.

How can postsecondary educators help our teachers to get intercultural communication competence to go beyond "just good teaching"? What is "intercultural communication competence" (Spitzberg 1997) and how will this understanding help the effectiveness of multicultural classroom teachers? This concept was further elaborated by Spitzberg and Changnon (2009) to explain that competent people are able to appropriately and effectively adapt their verbal and nonverbal messages to the cultural context in which

NEW DIRECTIONS FOR TEACHING AND LEARNING • DOI: 10.1002/tl

they are involved. Furthermore, Wiseman (2002) added that competent individuals must have some knowledge about the other with whom they are communicating, be motivated to communicate, engage in appropriate and effective verbal and nonverbal behaviors, and become sensitive to cultural factors affecting the interpretation of messages. Thus, it is expected that training will foster the intercultural competence of ESL teachers.

Training the ESL Teacher.   Teachers in K–12 regular classrooms generally haven't received bilingual/ESL professional training in college and only three states, namely, New York, Arizona, and Florida, require ESL training for all teachers. However, experts believe that those who receive intercultural training have gained knowledge and confidence to face challenges (Paige and Goode 2009). A list of essential prerequisites for effectiveness in multicultural classrooms is available to help teachers (see Gordon and Browne 2012).

Institutions of higher education offer intercultural training for teachers who choose to pursue the ESL Post Baccalaureate Certification or Add-On certification. For example, to add this certification any teacher who holds a valid Type A, B, C, Level 1, 2, or 3 in Louisiana must complete four additional courses: Methods of Teaching English as a Second Language, Intercultural Communication, Introduction to Linguistics, and Curriculum Design for Teaching English as a Second Language.

At the international level, another way to expose teachers to intercultural perspectives is to get them in contact with international faculty. The next section describes a few insights I had as international faculty member while training these teachers.

Being an International Faculty Member in the United States.   Hiring international faculty members with a PhD from US institution is becoming common and accelerates intercultural exposure. For example, when I came to the United States (from South America) for my first graduate degree two decades ago, I was the only international student in my classes, and only the second international student in the program. The path to that master's degree was lonely. Shared meaning with classmates was almost impossible, except for two friendly American classmates who already had experience with corporate expatriates. They were my source of social support. There were no international faculty members in that department. After graduation, and a few years later, I returned to America to pursue a doctoral degree. At that time I had four international classmates and still no international instructors in the program. However, I was able to share perceptions and experiences with other internationals. Currently, the proportion of international students and faculty is increasing rapidly in graduate programs. This generates intercultural learning, but to benefit from such interactions, students and teachers need to be open, receptive, and aware of the dynamics that exist in intercultural classrooms.

Classroom climates are rooted in cultural values, learning styles, teaching styles, and verbal and nonverbal communication (Skows and Stephan

2000). For example, cultural values and beliefs associated with "collectivism and individualism" may influence how a student behaves in a classroom. In individualistic societies (for example, United States) students speak up easily in class, while in most collectivistic societies (for example, Japan, China) students tend to believe that the young should learn and listen. Because of the less powerful role of the student in certain societies, students are encouraged to speak only when called upon. Additional variables impacting classroom dynamics are learning and teaching styles, verbal and nonverbal ways of speaking in the classroom, and rules of politeness and use of silence (Skows and Stephan 2000). In graduate school, I was surprised to observe American students eating snacks in class and speaking up concerning whatever thought that crossed their minds. This was in contrast to the classroom environment to which I had been previously exposed, where students would prefer to speak up only when they had a significant contribution to the class. Reflective thinking and formality was a must!

Teaching Intercultural Communication to Teachers: A Pilot Study

I have been working with ESL certification seekers for years while teaching this required intercultural class. This online course helps teachers from other areas of the state also obtain their certifications.

In this second section, I report my student–teachers' expectations, experiences, and insights about intercultural pedagogy, multicultural classroom dynamics, and interpretations of learned concepts. From here on I juxtapose academic style with a short section of freestyle writing in the last section of the chapter containing my reflections as found in autoethnographic studies (Cresswell 2007; Ellis 2004).

Information regarding demographics of these teachers and the data about their pupils' school levels can be found in the methods section. I also requested their opinions about the best delivery mode for this class (100 percent online, 50 percent online, face-to-face lectures, or other method). In addition, I asked for opinions regarding whether or not culturally and linguistically diverse instructors should be more equipped to teach intercultural classes (and why or why not?). Reports are in the results section.

Based on previously stated purposes the following research questions guided the pilot study:

RQ1: What are the teachers' expectations and experiences regarding the impact of this intercultural communication course on their teaching and classroom dynamics?
RQ2: What are the teachers' perceptions about the impact of acquired intercultural communication competence on their professional and personal lives?

Method.   The sample was composed of twenty ESL female student–teachers ($N = 20$) selected randomly during three semesters. All were seeking the ESL certification and ranged in age from twenty-six to fifty years. Participants also ranged from one to thirty-one years of teaching experience. They were all Caucasians, except for one Hispanic American female who came to the United States from Puerto Rico as a child. Considering grade levels and approximate age of the children, twelve responded that they were teaching elementary school, one was teaching middle school, one was teaching junior high, and one said she was teaching high school. The remaining five participants did not reveal what grade they were teaching.

Data were collected during three semesters. I report here participants' comments according to sequence posed by the research questions. I chose conversation analysis (Frey et al. 1992) to examine transcripts of conversations among participants and instructor and assignments in Blackboard platform. After cleaning the data, I reexamined the transcripts, and added my insights related to participants' comments in the final section.

The Discussion Board on Blackboard site was especially helpful because it gave teachers opportunities to exchange experiences, learn from one another, and develop shared understanding. Then, I categorized responses from assignments, organizing themes.

Results.   Two main thematic stipulations that emerged from the data were: (a) "Course Expectations and Applications" and (b) "Teaching and Intercultural Competence." Teachers' comments about each theme are organized below. There seems to be a common underlying drive among the twenty teachers relating to helping ESL students fulfill their educational needs so as to be later integrated in regular classrooms, and to understanding the dynamics of multicultural classrooms.

Course Expectations and Applications.   These teachers commented on the ethnic composition of their ESL classes: Taiwanese, Vietnamese, Indian, Pakistani, and Hispanics (mainly from Mexico, Puerto Rico, and Honduras). Participants claimed that as ESL teachers they intrinsically had special interest in other cultures and languages. This is the main reason they decided to become ESL teachers.

About 70 percent of participants were impressed by students' cultural values related to authority and hierarchy. The importance of respect for authority figures was evident in Hispanic and Asian ESL children and their parents. Having contact with people from other areas of the world make teachers realize the importance of respect for authority in other cultures while making them more enthusiastic, appreciative, and curious about those cultures' values. In fact, some participants highlighted that they learned to be respectful of other cultures as well: "Asian and Hispanic students have a much stronger upbringing, and one reason is that the children and parents are very respectful of the teachers" (Cindy, third grade teacher). Another participant added: "... and the importance of respect in those cultures made me even more enthusiastic about Asia" (Mary, fourth grade teacher). A first grade teacher mentioned: "in the last 5 years I have grown to love this type of student because they are very respectful in the classroom, which makes teaching them a pleasure most days." By understanding the cultural value of respect, teachers later learned that they and their ESL students have completely different definitions for class participation.

Most teachers had positive expectations regarding intercultural training impact on their teaching, professional, personal lives. Their comments were replete with teachers' new resolutions and propositions based on skills acquired and that would impact on a new pedagogy for their multicultural classrooms. Teachers expressed how exactly they were going to apply their new skills to bridge the gap between themselves and students. Their sensitivity and awareness had increased by the end of academic semester. Here are examples of positive expectations on personal and professional lives:

> I never imagined that understanding the concepts of intercultural communication would be helpful to me in many other areas of life. It broadens knowledge of the world and of oneself. Now, I dream of taking a trip abroad... dream about how to alleviate problems facing diverse students, how to work with limited English proficient students, and how to help them feel secure so they can succeed socially and academically. (ESL teacher, fifth grade)

Additional positive expectations related to US teachers and students' issues of engagement, tolerance, and global awareness: "I will be able to understand communication styles of these students, to get them more comfortable, involved, and help American-born students to appreciate many cultures, to make them aware of how this appreciation may help them communicate globally" (ESL French teacher, junior high, twenty years of experience). Another teacher reflected: "I learned about the culture of others but most importantly, I learned about my own US culture, became a more sensitive teacher" (ESL teacher, one-year experience).

Teaching and Intercultural Competence.   Teachers expressed how they plan to apply intercultural competence in their classrooms, revealed complete satisfaction with self-accomplishments and the accomplishments of their ESL students: "While taking this course I had twenty-two ESL learners, and am proud of my new acquired skills and the skills of my students. They achieved incredible growth in language acquisition and core curriculum in just one year's time, ... it is a HUGE reward to me as a teacher" (second grade, ESL teacher).

However, despite many positive feelings, some participants reported apprehension about future teacher–parents conferences. Such feelings of uncertainty and anxiety are common in unknown situations. A first grade teacher expressed her concern: "I am worried that I may offend the parents in some way, or that the gist of what I am saying will be lost in translation through a third party."

In sum, they unanimously reported that pursuing this certification was a smart decision. Intercultural learning made them aware of the role culture and language play in communication. Ultimately, their primary objective was to become better teachers, to meet students' learning needs, and to make students' experiences both productive and enjoyable.

To collect teachers' opinions on course design I asked two questions: (1) what is the best teaching method to cover intercultural topics in this course (100 percent online, 50 percent online, face-to-face/lectures, other)? (2) Should only culturally and linguistically diverse instructors teach intercultural courses/topics to US students? Why? Why not? Respondents to question 1 were divided: some still prefer face-to-face interactions while others preferred either a hybrid course or to continue with 100 percent NET. A person who preferred 100 percent face-to-face classes gave her reason: "this mode leads to deeper feelings of comfort in asking cultural questions that we can truly learn from."

Participants believed the best option for ESL intercultural classes possibly would be hybrid (face-to-face and NET mode; 50 percent of each). Additional suggestions included interactional and visual components (additional Skype interactions, chats with international students).

Responses to question 2 revealed the ideal instructor as someone "truly" able to relate to intercultural situations. I probed further by asking: "Are there disadvantages for a person who is not culturally and linguistically diverse to teach intercultural communication?" A middle school teacher promptly reacted: "Yes, because someone who is really diverse can outperform someone who is not. I am a bilingual ESL teacher, and can relate to ESL students and families easily compared to another ESL teacher who is not bilingual. Not knowing their language will impact on how they relate to this teacher."

Discussion.   The importance of acquiring intercultural skills is crucial and intercultural competence should continue as a mandatory part of curriculum to achieve the ESL certification. This pilot study explored expectations and experiences of teachers and how this new knowledge may impact their professional and personal lives. One limitation of the study is the generalization of results due to limitations of sampling procedures. It is possible that teachers who chose to pursue this certification are more sensitive to cultural differences than the general population of teachers. If I had replicated the study with teachers who were not seeking the certification I might have obtained different results. Possibly, the demographics of participants' in this geographic area (that is, females in the South) may have triggered specific results. My participants' strategies to effectively and appropriately teach

ESL students confirmed strategies recommended to multicultural teachers by Gordon and Browne (2012). They consider crucial for better understanding that such teachers need to learn all they can about the families of their ESL students; this helps to recognize and comprehend their value system.

Reflections of an International Instructor and Researcher

By looking at the teachers' elaborations on what was meaningful to them I share the resonances those stories had for me. My interest for intercultural communication began at an early age, watching effective coordination of languages and efforts among "foreign" engineers from a multinational organization, including my father, planning and implementing large machinery transportation from one country to another. In the same fashion, these teachers were learning intercultural communication by observing and living intercultural situations. By looking at teachers' comments, we realize that they are the foundation, helping to build a future workforce that will depend on effective cross-cultural communication to be productive.

I believe that schools and teachers need to continuously strive to create inclusive classrooms and programs that also lead to global awareness. ESL students need to immerse themselves in the culture and language of the geographic area in which their parents chose to live. To accelerate the process teachers who are culturally sensitive and prepared can take the role of facilitators. Domestic students can benefit from this process as well by learning about globalization, becoming prepared for the global workforce. Tolerance inside and outside of classrooms may increase by exposure to other perspectives of "doing" and "being" while learning perspective taking (placing oneself in the other person's shoes). Probably, this will take longer in some areas of the United States compared to other areas and countries. It is important to note that the new wave of immigrants to the United States is coming from collectivistic societies (Latin American, Asia). Teachers with intercultural competence skills will quickly realize this and incorporate the experiences of these cultures into their teaching repertoire.

References

Bernardo, M. A. C., and S. Malakolunthu. 2013. "Culturally-Inclusive Behavior of Filipino Teachers in International Schools in the Philippines: Perspectives of International Education in a Developing Country." *International Journal of Educational Development* 33: 59–64.

Bowman, N. A. 2010. "College Diversity Experiences and Cognitive Development: A Meta-Analysis." *Review of Educational Research* 80 (1): 4–33.

Cresswell, J. W. 2007. *Research Design: Qualitative, Quantitative, and Mixed-Methods Approach*, 3rd ed. Thousand Oaks, CA: Sage.

Education Week. 2009. *Quality Counts*. Accessed January 20, 2009. http://www.edweek .org/ew/toc/2009/01/08/index.html.

Ellis, C. 2004. *The Ethnographic I: A Methodological Novel about Ethnography*. Walnut Creek, CA: Altamira Press.

Frey, L. R., C. H. Botan, P. G. Friedman, and G. L. Kreps. 1992. *Interpreting Communication Research: A Case Study Approach*. Englewood Cliffs, NJ: Prentice-Hall.

Gopal, A. 2011. "Internationalization of Higher Education: Preparing Faculty to Teach Cross-Culturally." *International Journal of Teaching and Learning in Higher Education* 23 (3): 373–381.

Gordon, A. M., and K. Browne. 2012. *Beginning Essentials in Early Childhood Education*, 2nd ed. Belmont, CA: Cengage Learning.

Johnson, R. 1995. "ESL Teacher Education and Intercultural Communication: Discomfort as a Learning Tool." *TESL Canada Journal* 12 (2). http://teslcanadajournal .ca/index.php/tesl/issue/view/80.

McCall, A. L., and B. Vang. 2012. "Preparing Pre-Service Teachers to Meet the Needs of Hmong Refugee Students." *Multicultural Perspectives* 14 (1): 32–37.

McGray, D. 2006. "Lost in America." *Foreign Policy* 2006 (May/June): 40–48.

Merryfield, M. M., and M. Kasay. 2004. "How Are Teachers Responding to Globalization." *Social Education* 68 (5): 354–359.

Orfield, G., and M. Kurlaender. 2001. *Diversity Challenged: Evidence on the Impact of Affirmative Action*. Cambridge, MA: Harvard Educational Publishing Group.

Paige, R. M., and M. J. Goode. 2009. "Cultural Mentoring: International Education Professionals and the Development of Intercultural Competence." In *The Sage Handbook of Intercultural Competence*, edited by D. K. Deardorff, 333–349. Thousand Oaks, CA: Sage.

Skows, L. M., and L. Stephan. 2000. "Intercultural Communication in the Classroom." In *Intercultural Communication: A Reader*, edited by L. Samovar and R. Porter, 9th ed., 330–342. Boston, MA: Wadsworth.

Spitzberg, B. H. 1997. "A Model of Intercultural Competence." In *Intercultural Communication Reader*, edited by L. A. Samovar and R. E. Porter, 8th ed., 379–391. Belmont, CA: Wadsworth.

Spitzberg, B. H., and G. Changnon. 2009. "Conceptualizing Intercultural Competence." In *The Sage Handbook of Intercultural Communication Competence*, edited by D. K. Deardorff, 2–52. Thousand Oakes, CA: Sage.

Villegas, A. M., and T. Lucas. 2007. "The Culturally Responsive Teacher." *Educational Leadership* 64 (6): 28–33.

Wiseman, R. 2002. "Intercultural Communication Competence." In *Handbook of International and Intercultural Communication*, edited by W. B. Gudykunst and B. Mody, 2nd ed., 207–224. Thousand Oaks, CA: Sage.

Claudia L. McCalman is an associate professor in the Department of Languages and Communication, Southeastern Louisiana University.

New Directions for Teaching and Learning • DOI: 10.1002/tl

8

Using a combination of critical theory, poststructuralism, and critical pedagogy, this chapter calls for a shift in the ways we conceive, imagine, and represent international instructors in US classrooms. More specifically, it highlights the importance of the voices of international instructors themselves, proposes a shift from the current discourse of deficit to one of cultural wealth, and offers some directions for future research in this area.

Talking Back: Shifting the Discourse of Deficit to a Pedagogy of Cultural Wealth of International Instructors in US Classrooms

Gust A. Yep

Introduction

> Moving from silence into speech is for the oppressed, the colonized, the exploited, and those who stand and struggle side by side a gesture of defiance that heals, that makes life and new growth possible. It is that act of speech, of "talking back," that is no mere gesture of empty words, that is the expression of our movement from object to subject—the liberated voice.
>
> bell hooks (1989, 9)

The chapters in this volume represent the voices of international instructors in US classrooms "talking back." Navigating diverse cultural,

Portions of this chapter were presented at the "Toward Greater Community: Acknowledging the Community of Nonnative English-Speaking (NNES) Professors in the US Classroom" panel that Dr. Katherine G. Hendrix organized for the 98th Annual Meeting of the National Communication Association, Orlando, FL, November 2012. I dedicate this chapter to two truly remarkable and engaged educators: Dr. Rama Kased for our ongoing conversations about anti-oppressive education and Dr. Nancy McDermid for our continuing dialogue about teaching with love. In addition, I am grateful to my canine friends Yogi ("the Yogster"), my sweet and affectionate Pomeranian companion, and Rocky ("Fat Mosca"), an exuberant Pomeranian/sheltie mix, who, together, encourage me to "talk back" and engage the world with youthful innocence and enthusiasm. Finally, I thank my friend Craig Lange for his sense of humor and companionship in our city walks during the period of preparation of this chapter.

professional, and personal paths from Africa (Chapter 5), Asia (Chapters 1, 3, 4, and 6), Europe (Chapter 2), and South America (Chapter 7) to classrooms in various regions of the United States, these courageous walkers[1] bring new knowledges, skills, connectivities, and perspectives to US American college students. Inhabiting a range of social locations and narrating their pedagogical experiences in a variety of courses on various communication contexts, these authors document some of the journeys international instructors travel to become a member of the US professoriate. In this chapter, I examine some of the common themes highlighted by these walkers and offer some suggestions for reframing current cultural discourses of international instructors in US classrooms. To do so, the chapter is divided into three sections. "Mapping" retraces the steps of these walkers. "Remapping" calls for a shift from the current deficit model to a discourse of cultural wealth. In addition to briefly reflecting on my own journey from international teaching assistant (ITA) to tenured full professor in the US academy, "Walking" explores some potential directions for future research.

Mapping: Common Themes in "Talking Back"

Retracing the steps of these international instructors in US classrooms gives us an opportunity to understand their cultural journeys, learn from their pedagogical practices, appreciate their successes and challenges, and hopefully apply their knowledges and perspectives to transform ourselves as teachers and our classrooms as spaces of radical possibility. Such steps also provide a platform for us to witness and explore the dynamics of power, both macrocultural (for example, social institutions and cultural discourses) and microcultural (for example, teacher–student interactions), in US culture, particularly in its educational systems. The chapters exemplify, in many ways, engaged pedagogy, that is, teaching practices in which teachers are "actively committed to a process of self-actualization that promotes their own well-being if they are to teach in a manner that empowers students" (hooks 1994, 15). To empower our students is to engage in education as "the practice of freedom" by respecting and caring for their souls as well as our own and teaching in a way that "anyone can learn" (hooks 1994, 13). In short, engaged pedagogy empowers both students and teachers. This process of empowerment creates an atmosphere for students and teachers to learn from each other and subverts popular assumptions that students learn from teachers but teachers do not have anything to learn from students. Three themes emerged from the chapters in this volume: (a) teaching as a labor of love, (b) sharing of good teaching practices, and (c) documenting the lived experiences of international instructors through qualitative methodologies.

All the chapters in this volume, either explicitly or implicitly, discuss conscious teaching, or in hooks's (2010) words, "teaching with love" (160). One way of doing so is by reading and attending to the emotional climate of the students in the classroom, which requires teachers to be open, vulnerable, courageous, and respectful. Chen (Chapter 1), for example, discusses ways to create and maintain an atmosphere in which students, in her large introduction to intercultural communication course, have multiple venues to engage with her and her teaching assistant on challenging intercultural topics (for example, race and racism, the murder of Trayvon Martin). Through this ongoing engagement, Chen and her assistant blogged and reflected on the emotional climate of the students as well as her own emotional responses to the process of (re)racialization as an Asian woman in the classroom. As a Kenyan woman speaking British English in US classrooms, Mutua (Chapter 5) discusses how she acknowledges and works with students who question her linguistic competence. By acknowledging students' linguistic attitudes and prejudices, she increases students' understanding of multiple English dialects in the world as well as creating a more open classroom climate. Similarly, Kittler (Chapter 2) reflects on his reactions and responses to a student revolt in his Magazine Editing class when he attempted to provide important historical and philosophical context in addition to practical skills. Recognizing different emotional responses to his course material—those of his students and colleagues as well as his own—enabled him to see cultural differences in education and pervasive neoliberal practices in the US academy. In short, teaching with love is about engaging with, and not running away from, emotional challenges and topics, and "having the clarity to know what to do on any day to create the best climate for optimal learning" (hooks 2010, 161) for both students and teachers.

A second theme emerging from the narratives in this volume is the sharing of good teaching practices in US classrooms. Such practices are, in my view, important and useful pedagogical approaches in any classroom regardless of subject matter, classroom size, or student population. They include: development of good teacher–student rapport; cultivation of open and positive attitudes toward students; investment in students' growth and success; and teacher's preparation, confidence, and concern for student learning, among others. For example, Zhang (Chapter 3) explores ways to enhance teacher student rapport through understanding, openness, role modeling, and managing proper communication space. Similarly, Hsu (Chapter 4) discusses ways of fostering open and positive attitudes in the classroom through the use of confirming behaviors that validate students' perceptions, behaviors, and identities. Focusing on students' growth and academic success, McCalman (Chapter 7) examines ways to increase cultural competence for students pursuing the English as a Second Language (ESL) certification. In her autoethnographical reflections, Hebbani (Chapter 6) takes us through her multiple journeys from ITA to university professor. Such journeys include effective reactions (for example, excitement, anxiety), cognitive concerns (for example, intelligibility of accents, clarity of presentation), and behavioral practices (for example, punctuality, preparation) as she continued to refine her own pedagogical style for diverse student populations. Finally, Hebbani and Hendrix (Chapter 6) examine the experiences and practices of ITAs in the Oral Communication classroom at various US American institutions. Together, these authors provide us with rich theoretical and pragmatic pedagogical insights into teaching in undergraduate US classrooms. They also show us the potential of engaged pedagogy that, in hooks's (1994) words, "values student expression" (20).

Another theme emerging from the chapters is the use of qualitative methods to document the voices and experiences of the international instructors contributing to this volume. As Hendrix and Hebbani note in their introduction as well as in all the chapters included in this volume, qualitative methods are particularly appropriate for capturing the nuances and intricacies of the lived experiences—in all of their complexities, consonances, dissonances, and fragmentations—of people, particularly those who have been hidden and unintelligible in the US higher educational landscape. Autoethnographic accounts, for example, are particularly important for exploring the connections between the individual (for example, personal experiences in the classroom) and the social (for example, the social and cultural conditions that inform and influence personal experiences and interactions) where cultural identities are in ongoing negotiation, contestation, and renegotiation (Yep 2004).

Remapping: Toward a Pedagogy of Cultural Wealth

In addition to their general invisibility in the pedagogical literature (see Editors' Notes of this volume), international instructors are typically viewed as deficient, that is, lacking in knowledge and skills—linguistic, social, and cultural, among others—to teach in US classrooms. In other words, the dominant cultural discourse about international instructors is their lack of cultural and pedagogical competence. Such discourse subscribes to an underlying logic of "deficit thinking" that maintains, reinforces, and perpetuates social hierarchies and normativities—based on race, class, gender, sexuality, nation, and the body, among others—in US culture (García and Guerra 2004, 154). Although some of the chapters in this volume move away from deficit thinking, others implicitly subscribe to it. By deconstructing how such thinking implicitly or explicitly marginalizes—in fact, degrades and pathologizes—difference, US dynamics of cultural domination and subordination can be illuminated. It is obvious, for example, to see who is marginalized when international instructors are viewed as deficient and incompetent. However, it might be much less apparent to discern what race, class, gender, sexuality, nation, and bodily hierarchies and normativities are tacitly—and perhaps not so tacitly—upheld and celebrated in the process. To understand this opacity, it is important to ask some critical questions: Who benefits from deficit thinking? What are the discursive and material mechanisms that sustain it? How can it be subverted?

NEW DIRECTIONS FOR TEACHING AND LEARNING • DOI: 10.1002/tl

Another way of viewing difference—one that does not automatically cast the international instructor as a "problem" in educational settings—is by conceiving and treating it as a vital aspect of social and cultural realities in the global world. Recognizing that racism and other "-isms" are disguised in the rhetoric of the normative—consider the "-isms" implicated in the trope of the "normal person" or the "average US American"—and viewing difference as an asset rather than a liability, Yosso (2005) proposed the notion of "cultural wealth" for understanding the resources, histories, and lives of US students of color (69). Adopting this approach to international instructors, I call for a shift from the current discourse of deficit to one of cultural wealth in US educational institutions.

Cultural wealth refers to "an array of knowledge, skills, abilities and contacts" (Yosso 2005, 77) that international instructors possess and utilize to survive and resist cultural normativities and to succeed and thrive in US classrooms. In essence, cultural wealth refers to unrecognized forms of capital that international instructors bring to US classrooms and educational institutions. They include linguistic, aspirational, familial, social, navigational, resistant, and informational capital (Liou, Antrop-González, and Cooper 2009; Yosso 2005). Further, Yosso (2005) reminds us, "these various forms of capital are not mutually exclusive or static, but rather are dynamic processes that build on one another as part of community cultural wealth" (77). I now turn to discuss these forms of capital in relationship to international instructors in US educational environments.

Linguistic capital refers worldviews and skills associated with communication in more than one language and/or style. For example, international instructors are likely to be multilingual, which allows them to bring multiple worldviews and linguistic skills to the US American students they encounter in the classroom. Aspirational capital includes goals and dreams for the future in spite of personal and structural barriers. Clearly, international instructors have high hopes and aspirations (for example, ITAs working on their doctorate degrees), which can be used to inspire students in the classroom and beyond. Familial capital is not necessarily about kinship relations and includes cultural knowledges that maintain a sense of cultural identity, history, and memory for a group. As individuals and groups from different cultures, international instructors internationalize the US American university with their embodied knowledge of multiple cultural systems. Social capital refers to networks of people, including interpersonal and intercultural connections, in a global world. International instructors are likely to internationalize the social contacts and networks for students and the institution they are working for. Navigational capital is about the ability to maneuver through social institutions (for example, educational systems, government agencies) that were not necessarily created with international instructors in mind. Undoubtedly, for them to be teaching in US classrooms, they already have successful experiences (for example, getting admitted to graduate school, obtaining a visa) of navigating these institutions, which can become a rich resource for students and university programs.

Resistant capital includes embodied knowledges and everyday practices of living in a culture that is not necessarily appreciative or celebratory of the international instructors' cultural identities. The ongoing adaptations these instructors make in their new environments become a reservoir of wisdom that is valuable for surviving and thriving in a multicultural world. Finally, informational capital refers to knowledge networks that are essential for academic success, such as informal information that provides constant encouragement and motivation for international instructors to continue their academic and pedagogical achievements. Taken together, these multiple, dynamic, and interrelated forms of capital—linguistic, aspirational, familial, social, navigational, resistant, and informational (Liou et al. 2009; Yosso 2005)—endow international instructors with enormous cultural wealth that benefit US American students and institutions.

A pedagogy of cultural wealth recognizes, values, and engages the various forms of capital that international instructors bring to US classrooms. Consistent with the tenets of Critical Race Theory (CRT), a pedagogy of cultural wealth is characterized by five important features (Yosso 2005). First, it highlights the importance of intersectionality, based on race, class, gender, sexuality, nation, and the body, among others, as simultaneous vectors of privilege and subordination (see, for example, Jones and Calafell 2012; Yep 2013, forthcoming). Second, it challenges dominant cultural ideologies, such as color blindness and neoliberalism (see, for example, Giroux 2007; Jones and Calafell 2012). Third, it recognizes the importance of experiential and cultural knowledges, including local and culturally specific ways of knowing (see, for example, Asante 2014; Miike 2014). Fourth, it embraces a transdisciplinary perspective to produce multiple worldviews and approaches to a subject, such as different ways of understanding and exploring silence (see, for example, Yep and Shimanoff 2013; Yosso 2005). Finally, it is committed to social justice, equality, and personal and collective empowerment and liberation (see, for example, hooks 1994, 2010; Yosso 2005). In short, a pedagogy of cultural wealth is committed to hooks's (1994) vision of "education as the practice of freedom" (6) that I discussed earlier.

Walking: Directions for Future Research

The process of listening to the authors in this volume "talk back" to register their presence and intelligibility in the pedagogical literature triggered memories of my own journey to the US professoriate. As an "Asianlatinoamerican" (Yep 2002, 60), who lived in multiple cultural contexts, came to the United States to pursue higher education that culminated in a doctorate degree, and later shifted my paradigmatic orientation from postpositivist to critical and poststructuralist, I found convergences and divergences in the paths we have walked. I am multilingual—English, Spanish, and Chinese, in order of proficiency—and I speak all three languages with a slight accent, which I view as my own linguistic capital rather than a deficit that I need to compensate for (Yep 2002). After completing high school at 15 and finishing my undergraduate degree several years later, I started out as a young ITA teaching various introductory courses. During my itinerary from ITA to lecturer at my doctoral institution, I was reminded, more than once, that I was the only international instructor who was "allowed" to teach his own stand-alone courses. Although I felt fortunate, I was also acutely aware of my non-normativities through the silences and the silencing of my multiple identities in graduate school. But I never really felt deficient. Through a lengthy journey full of hope and anxiety, optimism and fear, excitement and insecurity, calm and anger, understanding and confusion, confidence and doubt, I came to accept—and embrace, thanks, in part, to bell hooks's (1989, 1990, 1994, 2010, 2013) writings, particularly those about marginality as a site of radical possibility—that my identities are forever marked in the academy and in US culture. As a queer-identified person of color challenging hegemonic heteropatriarchal masculinity in my "everyday practices," to invoke de Certeau's (1984, xix) words, my identities are nonnormative, and, therefore, marked in US culture at this historical juncture. After being granted early tenure at two different institutions and receiving early promotion to full professor at my current institution, I continue negotiating my multiple identities in the classroom as I teach emotionally challenging subjects (for example, culture, race, gender, sexuality) and mentor diverse students (for example, normative and nonnormative social locations and identifications) from the perspective of cultural wealth.

To conclude, I offer some suggestions for future research on international instructors in US classrooms. As more international instructors "talk back" and share the paths they walked, it is important, in my view, to focus on several things. First, it is critical to explore these journeys from a perspective of "thick intersectionalities," that is, how race, class, gender, sexuality, nation, and the body, among others, come together simultaneously to produce particular identities and experiences in the US academy and beyond (Yep 2013, 123). A thick intersectional perspective proposes that such explorations struggle against coherence and premature closure of identity, embrace the messiness of everyday experiences, focus on the affective investments that people make on their identity performances, and attempt to make sense of identities as embodied and lived by people within specific geopolitical and historical contexts (Yep, forthcoming). Second, it is important to explore the role and experience of affect in these journeys. Engaged pedagogy focuses on the entire person—mind, body, heart, and soul—involved in the pedagogical relationship, which includes both teachers and students. At the same time, engaged instructors are responsive to the emotional climate of the students and are committed to the well-being of students as well as their own (hooks 1994, 2010). Third, it is critical to examine how neoliberalism and the increasing commodification of knowledge in the United States have produced new perspectives on education and new modes of suffering. Such suffering includes, among others, the ongoing assault on academic freedom through the corporatization of the university, the continuing "militarization of higher education," and the mounting loan debt that our students incur as higher education becomes increasingly out of reach to larger segments of the US population (Giroux 2007, 18). Kittler (Chapter 2 of this volume), for example, highlights the current US American demand for practicality at the expense of contextualized and deep understanding, which profoundly influences our curricular content, relationship with students, and the future of institutions of higher learning. Finally, it is important for international instructors to recognize, embrace, and document the cultural wealth they bring to US classrooms. By engaging in a pedagogy of cultural wealth, international instructors can expand minds and hearts and enrich souls and spirits, including those of students as well as their own, and transform their teaching into what bell hooks (2010) calls "a prophetic vocation" (181).

Note

1. I contend that international instructors are, in many ways, like de Certeau's (1984) "walkers" navigating a social landscape (92). Walkers are practitioners who simultaneously influence culture (for example, contesting cultural stereotypes, internationalizing the university) and are shaped by larger macrostructures of power (for example, cultural discourses of immigrants, educational systems) as they engage in the daily practices of life (for example, teaching, mentoring). Such practices have the potential to reify and maintain, resist and transgress, and change and transform hegemonic power structures.

References

Asante, M. K. 2014. "Afrocentricity: Toward a New Understanding of African Thought in the World." In *The Global Intercultural Communication Reader*, edited by M. F. Asante, Y. Miike, and J. Yin, 2nd ed., 101–110. New York, NY: Routledge.

de Certeau, M. 1984. *The Practice of Everyday Life*. Translated by S. Rendall. Berkeley, CA: University of California Press.

García, S. B., and P. L. Guerra. 2004. "Deconstructing Deficit Thinking: Working with Educators to Create More Equitable Learning Environments." *Education and Urban Society* 35 (2): 150–168.

Giroux, H. A. 2007. *The University in Chains: Confronting the Military–Industrial– Academic Complex*. Boulder, CO: Paradigm.

hooks, b. 1989. *Talking Back: Thinking Feminist, Thinking Black*. Boston, MA: South End Press.

hooks, b. 1990. *Yearning: Race, Gender, and Cultural Politics*. Boston, MA: South End Press.

hooks, b. 1994. *Teaching to Transgress: Education as the Practice of Freedom*. New York, NY: Routledge.

hooks, b. 2010. *Teaching Critical Thinking: Practical Wisdom*. New York, NY: Routledge.

hooks, b. 2013. *Writing Beyond Race: Living Theory and Practice*. New York, NY: Routledge.

Jones, R. G., and B. M. Calafell. 2012. "Contesting Neoliberalism through Critical Pedagogy, Intersectional Reflexivity, and Personal Narrative: Queer Tales of Academia." *Journal of Homosexuality* 59: 957–981.

Liou, D. D., R. Antrop-González, and R. Cooper. 2009. "Unveiling the Promise of Community Cultural Wealth to Sustaining Latina/o Students' College-Going Information Networks." *Educational Studies* 45: 534–555.

Miike, Y. 2014. "The Asiacentric Turn in Asian Communication Studies: Shifting Paradigms and Changing Perspectives." In *The Global Intercultural Communication Reader*, edited by M. F. Asante, Y. Miike, and J. Yin, 2nd ed., 111–133. New York, NY: Routledge.

Yep, G. A. 2002. "My Three Cultures: Navigating the Multicultural Identity Landscape." In *Readings in Intercultural Communication: Experiences and Contexts*, edited by J. N. Martin, T. K. Nakayama, and L. A. Flores, 60–66. Boston, MA: McGraw-Hill.

Yep, G. A. 2004. "Approaches to Cultural Identity: Personal Notes from an Autoethnographical Journey." In *Communicating Ethnic and Cultural Identity*, edited by M. Fong and R. Chuang, 69–81. Lanham, MD: Rowman & Littlefield.

Yep, G. A. 2013. "Queering/Quaring/Kauering/Crippin'/Transing 'Other Bodies' in Intercultural Communication." *Journal of International and Intercultural Communication* 6 (2): 118–126.

Yep, G. A. Forthcoming. "Toward Thick(er) Intersectionalities: Theorizing, Researching, and Activating the Complexities of Communication and Identities." In *Globalizing Intercultural Communication: A Reader*, edited by K. Sorrells and S. Sekimoto. Thousand Oaks, CA: Sage.

Yep, G. A., and S. B. Shimanoff. 2013. "The U.S. Day of Silence: Sexualities, Silences, and the Will to Unsay in the Age of Empire." In *Silence, Feminism, Power: Reflections at the Edges of Sound*, edited by S. Malhotra and A. Carrillo Rowe, 139–156. London, UK: Palgrave Macmillan.

Yosso, T. J. 2005. "Whose Culture Has Capital? A Critical Race Theory Discussion of Community Cultural Wealth." *Race, Ethnicity and Education* 8 (1): 69–91.

GUST A. YEP *is a professor of communication studies, graduate faculty of sexuality studies, and faculty of the EdD program in educational leadership at San Francisco State University.*

NEW DIRECTIONS FOR TEACHING AND LEARNING • DOI: 10.1002/tl

INDEX

Abbott, R. D., 29
Academic Honor Council, 22
Albert, R. D., 1
Alibhai, N., 52
Allen, B. J., 61
Allen, M., 43
Al-Sharideh, K. A., 52
American Tongues, 35
Antrop-González, R., 87, 88
Ardener, S., 53, 54
Asante, M. K., 88
"Asian-ness," 10, 12, 14
Aspirational capital, 87
Autoethnography, 29–30
Axelson, E. R., 51

Bailey, K. M., 29, 52, 57
Ball, S. J., 21
Barnes, G. A., 29
Bazemore, S. D., 30
Bergerson, A. A., 52, 58
Bernardo, M. A. C., 73
Bitzer, L., 31
Bochner, A. P., 1, 18, 30, 52
Bok, D., 21
Botan, C. H., 77
Bowman, N. A., 74
Braun, J. L., 35
Bresnahan, M. J., 29
Brookfield, S. D., 6, 8
Brown, K., 51
Browne, K., 75, 80
Butler, J., 30

Cai, D. H., 29
Calafell, B. M., 88
Carbaugh, D., 7
Carlson, T. L., 35
Carr, D., 29
Causey, A., 5
Chalupa, C., 51
Chang, H., 30
Changnon, G., 74
Chase, S. E., 29
Chen, G.-M., 29
Chen, Y.-W., 5, 16, 85
Chesebro, J. D., 18

Chevalier, M., 19
Chism, N., 52
Chomsky, N., 25
Cooks, L. M., 5
Cooper, R., 87, 88
Cresswell, J. W., 76
Creswell, J. W., 62
Crites, S., 29
Critical Race Theory (CRT), 88
Cultural identity, 5–6; "Asian-ness,"
    10, 12; intersecting, 8–13; "Han-
    Chinese," 9. *See also* Identity
    negotiations
Cultural wealth, 87; pedagogy of, 86–88

Damron, J., 52
Davies, B., 18
de Certeau, M., 89, 90
de la Luz Reyes, M., 61
Denzin, N. K., 62
de Oliveira, E. A., 35
de Oliveira, S. G., 35
Derlega, V. J., 30
de Tocqueville, A., 19, 26
DeVoss, D., 7
Dinkha, J., 6, 7
Douglas, D., 32
Drzewiecka, J. A., 7

Ellis, C. S., 18, 30, 52, 76
Ellis, K., 43
Ellis, L., 30
English as a Second Language (ESL) cer-
    tification, 74, 85
ESL. *See* English as a Second Language
    (ESL) certification

Fassett, D. L., 9
Finger, G. A., 29
Fishman, P., 51
Fitch, F., 52
Floccia, C., 30
Foote, K. E., 5
Foreign Services Institute, 7–8
Frey, L. R., 77
Friedman, P. G., 77
Fryberg, S. A., 7

Frymier, A. B., 29, 43
Furnham, A., 52

Gao, X., 1
Garate, E. M., 57
García, S. B., 86
Gass, R. H., 34
Gergen, K. J., 29
Gergen, M. M., 29
Giles, H., 54
Giroux, H. A., 88, 90
Goe, W. R., 52
Goodboy, A. K., 43
Goode, M. L., 75
Gopal, A., 74
Gordon, A. M., 75, 80
Goslin, J., 30
Guerra, P. L., 86

Halcon, J. J., 61
Halualani, R. T., 7, 8
Hamilton, T., 19, 27
Hamlet, J. D., 7
Hao, R. N., 1
Hardgrove, T. D., 7
Harding, S., 17, 53
Harré, R., 18
Hart, W. B., 7
Hartsock, N., 53
Hayden, D., 7
Hebbani, A., 1, 2, 3, 61, 70, 85, 86
Hendrix, K. G., 1, 2, 3, 30, 52, 61, 70, 83, 86
Herman, E. S., 25
Hintikka, M. B., 17
Hoekje, B., 52, 58
Holland, B., 1
hooks, b., 83, 84, 85, 86, 88, 89, 90
Houser, M. L., 43
Houston, M., 61
Hsu, C.-F., 1, 2, 41, 43, 46, 49, 85
Humphreys, M. S., 63
Hymes, D. H., 62

Identity negotiations: critical reflections of, 8–13; among international faculty, 6–7; "othered," 12–13; overview, 5–6; racialized, 9–12; in teaching intercultural communication, 7–8
Intercultural communication competence: applications of, 77–78; applications of, in classroom, 78–79; importance of, to teachers, 76–80; in multicultural learning environment, 74–76; pilot study, 76–80
International faculty: attitudes of, toward teaching, 41–48; credibility of, 29–38; cultural wealth of, 83–90; and identity negotiations, 5–13; and intercultural communication competence, 73–80; overview, 1–2; and US educational system, 17–27
International instructors, credibility of, 29–38; knowledge demonstration, 34–36; openness, 32–33; overview, 29–31; presentation clarity, 34–35; rapport establishment, 31–34; reflections on, 36–38; relevant knowledge, 35–36; role modeling, 33; speech class challenges, 30–31; subject expertise, 34; understanding of student concerns, 31–32; use of communication space, 33–34
International Teaching Assistants (ITA), 1, 51–59, 61–69; African, 55–56; authoritarian style of, 57; autoethnographic reflections of, 67–69; current level of study on, 65; implications for, 58–59, 69; linguistic competence of, 54–55; muted group theory and, 53–54; overview, 51–52; qualitative research on, 62–67; standpoint theory and, 53; in US classroom, 52–53; and US education system, 56–58
ITA. See International Teaching Assistants (ITA)

Jackson, II, R. L., 1, 61
Janda, L. H., 30
Jasken, J., 7
Jia, C., 52, 58
Johnson, B. J., 7
Johnson, O., 1
Johnson, R., 74
Jones, N., 52
Jones, R. G., 88
Jones, S. H., 30
Ju, R., 1, 29, 30

Kasay, M., 74
Kased, R., 83
Keysar, B., 30

Kim, D., 5, 6, 7, 13
Kittler, J., 2, 17, 27, 85, 90
Knowledge demonstration, 34–36; presentation clarity, 34–35; relevant knowledge, 35–36; subject expertise, 34
Kozlova, I., 1
Kramarae, C., 53
Kreps, G. L., 77
Kuhn, E., 42
Kurlaender, M., 74

Lair, A., 51
Landa, M., 57
Lange, C., 83
Leeds-Hurtwitz, W., 8
Lev-Ari, S., 30
Li, L., 1, 29, 30
Li, W., 5
Lincoln, Y. S., 62
Linguistic capital, 87–88
Liou, D. D., 87, 88
Lippmann, W., 25
Liu, M., 1
Lucas, T., 74

Madden, C. G., 51
Malakolunthu, S., 73
Manrique, C. G., 6, 14
Manrique, G. G., 6, 14
Manufacturing Consent, 25
Martin, J. N., 7
Martin, T., 10, 11, 14, 85
Mazer, J. P., 1, 29, 30
McCall, A. L., 73
McCalman, C. L., 2, 5, 7, 43, 73, 81, 85
McCroskey, J. C., 29, 43
McDermid, N., 83
McGray, D., 73
Mendoza, S. L., 7
Merryfield, M. M., 74
Miike, Y., 88
Mohanty, S. P., 6, 7, 12, 14
Monk, J., 5
Mooz-lum, 10–11
Morgan, S. E., 52
Morse, J. M., 62
Multicultural learning environment, 74–76; ESL professional training, 75; international faculty member, 75–76
Muted group theory, 53–54

Mutua, C. N., 2, 51, 57, 60, 85
Myers, S. A., 43

Nakayama, T. K., 7, 8
Navigational capital, 87–88
New York Times, The, 22
Ngampornchai, A., 7
Nonnative-speaking instructors, recommendations for, 46–48
Nyquist, J. D., 29

Oetzel, J. G., 1
Office of Institutional Research, 8
Ogay, T., 54
Olivas, M. R., 61
Ono, K. A., 61
Open Doors Report, 5
Orbe, M. P., 53, 59, 61
Orfield, G., 73
Owen, W. F., 44

Paige, R. M., 75
Patton, T. O., 30
Paulson, J. F., 30
Pearson, F., 52
Perry, W., 57
Petrunia, M. D., 7
Pialorsi, F., 29
Pica, T., 29
Plakans, B. S., 51
Position, 18
Preiss, R. W., 43

Rapport establishment, 31–34; openness, 32–33; role modeling, 33; understanding of student concerns, 31–32; utilizing communication space, 33–34
Reed-Danahay, D., 1
Reflections, 6, 36–37; critical, 8–13; of international instructor, 80; of international teaching assistant, 67–69
Resistant capital, 88
Richard, M. G., 62
Richmond, V. P., 29
Rogers, E. M., 7
Root, E., 7

Sarkisian, E., 29
Schrodt, P., 43
Seiter, J. S., 34

Selinker, L., 52
Sellnow, D. D., 1
Shaw, P. A., 52, 57
Sheehan, O. T. O., 52
Shimanoff, S. B., 88
Simmons, N., 8, 9, 10, 11, 12, 13
Simpson, J. S., 5
Skows, L. M., 75, 76
Smith, A. E., 63
Smith, A. G., 7
Smith, D. E., 53
Soliz, J. S., 43
Spitzberg, B. H., 74
Sprague, J., 29
Spry, T., 1
Standpoint theory, 17, 18, 53, 56
Stephan, L., 75, 76

Takai, J., 1
Teaching: attitudes toward, 41–48; con-
firmation model of, 42–44; and inter-
cultural competence, 78–79; personal
experiences of, 41–42; recommenda-
tions for nonnative-speaking teach-
ers, 46–48; students' reactions to,
44–46
Teaching assistants (TA), 51
Teven, J. J., 31
Theobald, R., 5
Thomas, J. M., 7
Trebing, D., 1
Turman, P. D., 43
Twombly, S., 5, 6, 7, 13

US educational system, 18; and abstract forms of knowledge, 20–24;

college as restaurant, 21–22; historical European attitudes toward, 19–
20; nonnative teacher and, 24–26;
overview, 17–18; student as client,
22–23

Vang, B., 73
Van Langenhove, L., 18
Venette, S., 1
Villegas, A. M., 74

Wang, J., 43, 44, 47, 48
Warren, J. T., 9
Wheeless, L. R., 43
Wilcox, R. G., 1
Williams, J., 52, 58
Williams, L., 6
Winter, G., 22
Wiseman, R., 75
Wolf-Wendel, L., 5, 6, 7, 13
Wong (Lau), K., 1
Wood, J. T., 53, 56
Wright, S., 6, 7
Wulff, D. H., 29

Yep, G. A., 2, 83, 86, 88, 89, 91
Yook, E. L., 1
Yosso, T. J., 87, 88
Young, T. J., 29
Yule, G., 52

Zhai, L., 52
Zhang, M., 29, 39, 85
Zhang, Q., 1, 2
Zinn, H., 24, 25
Zukowski/Faust, J., 29

OTHER TITLES AVAILABLE IN THE
NEW DIRECTIONS FOR TEACHING AND LEARNING SERIES
Catherine M. Wehlburg, Editor-in-Chief
R. Eugene Rice, Consulting Editor

For a complete list of back issues, please visit www.josseybass.com/go/ndtl

TL137 **Active Learning Spaces**
Paul Baepler, D. Christopher Brooks, J. D. Walker, Editors
When we think about some of the main concepts that are embodied in the recent teaching and learning paradigm shift, we think about student engagement, active learning, collaboration, and peer instruction. And when we reflect upon the impediments to making these things happen in courses, instructors often indict the physical spaces in which they teach. The configuration of classrooms, the technology within them, and the behaviors they encourage are frequently represented as a barrier to enacting student—centered teaching methods, because traditionally designed rooms typically lack flexibility in seating arrangement, are configured to privilege a speaker at the front of the room, and lack technology to facilitate student collaboration. But many colleges and universities are redesigning the spaces in which students learn, collapsing traditional lecture halls and labs to create new, hybrid spaces—large technology-enriched studios—with the flexibility to support active and collaborative learning in larger class sizes. With this change, our classrooms are coming to embody the 21st-century pedagogy which many educators accept, and research and teaching practice are beginning to help us to understand the educational implications of thoughtfully engineered classrooms—in particular, that space and how we use it affects what, how, and how much students learn.
ISBN 978-11188-70112

TL136 **Doing the Scholarship of Teaching and Learning: Measuring Systematic Changes to Teaching and Improvements in Learning**
Regan A. R. Gurung, Janie H. Wilson, Editors
The Scholarship of Teaching and Learning (SoTL) should be an integral part of every academic's life, representing not only the pinnacle of effortful teaching, but also standing side by side with more conventional disciplinary scholarship. Although practiced by many instructors for years, SoTL has garnered national attention resulting in a spate of new journals to publish pedagogical research. SoTL helps students, fosters faculty development, and has been integrated into higher education in *Scholarship of Teaching and Learning Reconsidered* (Hutchings, Huber, & Ciccone, 2011). This volume provides readers with challenges that will motivate them to engage in SoTL and take their pedagogical research further. We include many key features aimed to help both the teacher new to research and SoTL and also researchers who may have a long list of scholarly publications in non-pedagogical areas and who have not conducted research.
ISBN 978-11188-38679

CHESAPEAKE COLLEGE
THE LIBRARY
WYE MILLS
MARYLAND 21679

NEW DIRECTIONS FOR TEACHING AND LEARNING
ORDER FORM SUBSCRIPTION AND SINGLE ISSUES

DISCOUNTED BACK ISSUES:

Use this form to receive 20% off all back issues of *New Directions for Teaching and Learning*.
All single issues priced at **$23.20** (normally $29.00)

TITLE	ISSUE NO.	ISBN

*Call 888-378-2537 or see mailing instructions below. When calling, mention the promotional code JBNND
to receive your discount. For a complete list of issues, please visit www.josseybass.com/go/ndtl*

SUBSCRIPTIONS: (1 YEAR, 4 ISSUES)

☐ New Order   ☐ Renewal

U.S.	☐ Individual: $89	☐ Institutional: $311
CANADA/MEXICO	☐ Individual: $89	☐ Institutional: $351
ALL OTHERS	☐ Individual: $113	☐ Institutional: $385

*Call 888-378-2537 or see mailing and pricing instructions below.
Online subscriptions are available at www.onlinelibrary.wiley.com*

ORDER TOTALS:

Issue / Subscription Amount: $ _____

Shipping Amount: $ _____
(for single issues only – subscription prices include shipping)

Total Amount: $ _____

SHIPPING CHARGES:	
First Item	$6.00
Each Add'l Item	$2.00

*(No sales tax for U.S. subscriptions. Canadian residents, add GST for subscription orders. Individual rate subscriptions must
be paid by personal check or credit card. Individual rate subscriptions may not be resold as library copies.)*

BILLING & SHIPPING INFORMATION:

☐ **PAYMENT ENCLOSED:** *(U.S. check or money order only. All payments must be in U.S. dollars.)*

☐ **CREDIT CARD:** ☐ VISA ☐ MC ☐ AMEX

Card number _____ Exp. Date _____

Card Holder Name _____ Card Issue # _____

Signature _____ Day Phone _____

☐ **BILL ME:** *(U.S. institutional orders only. Purchase order required.)*

Purchase order # _____
Federal Tax ID 13559302 • GST 89102-8052

Name _____

Address _____

Phone _____ E-mail _____

Copy or detach page and send to: **John Wiley & Sons, One Montgomery Street, Suite 1200,
San Francisco, CA 94104-4594**

Order Form can also be faxed to: **888-481-2665**

PROMO JBNND